The Bathroom Business Bible

Dedication

The seeds for the ideas presented in this book were planted
in my mind by the many fine business associates, clients,
competitors and friends I have been privileged to work
with in my business career to date.
This book is a tribute to you all.

However, this book is most especially dedicated to the
two people who gave me the values I hold dear and the
attitudes that make me who I am; who encouraged
my curiosity and development; and who continue to
inspire me by all that they are and all that they do
— Stella and John McCann —
my parents and best friends.

The Bathroom Business Bible

Deiric McCann

The Liffey Press

liffey press

Published by
The Liffey Press Ltd
Ashbrook House, 10 Main Street
Raheny, Dublin 5, Ireland
www.theliffeypress.com

Copyright © 2003 Deiric McCann

First Edition

ISBN 1-904148-41-7

Printed and bound in Spain by GraphyCems

ORDERING
Quantity Sales
Discounts are available to corporations or others purchasing in large quantities. For details please contact The Liffey Press at the address above.

Individual Sales
Liffey Press publications are available through all good bookstores, and directly from The Liffey Press (contact details above).

College textbook / course use; Orders by US trade bookstores and wholesalers
Please contact The Liffey Press (contact details above).

Copyediting, book design and layout by The Edit Room and PageWorks (emerryan@theeditroom.ie) (davidhoulden@eircom.net)
Original illustrations by Niall Murphy (niallkmurphy@eircom.net)
Jacket Design by MIG1 Design, Ireland (sean@mig1.com)
Cover photography by Hugh Glynn, Dublin (Tel: + 353 1 475 6038)

Contents

Contents

Introduction

Have you ever been faced by a business challenge that you couldn't immediately handle — one that you knew someone must have addressed previously, if only you had the opportunity to pick their brains? I have! In fact, one of the things I enjoy about being in business is the way you never quite know what's going to happen next, or how you're going to cope with it. I find that, however long I'm in business, there always seems to be a new challenge.

I've been pretty successful, and I've always felt that I'd be where I am now a whole lot faster if I had had some help in coping with the roadblocks that business life tends to throw in your path.

I wrote this book to provide you with the benefit of my experience. The book puts at your disposal forty strategies for coping with fundamental business challenges — the ones that, in my experience, tend to throw people of track unnecessarily. I've proven the effectiveness of every one of these strategies in my own business. They all share one thing in common — they work!

Now, I'm certainly not an academic, and so this book is not an academic treatise. It is filled with practical advice to help practical businesspeople to address practical business challenges. This is not a book that requires that you read it from page 1 to page 278. Put it in your briefcase, or on your desk, or even in your bathroom (!) — anywhere it'll be to hand when you have a few minutes to spare. You'll find that each of the forty strategies is self-contained and none of them will take you more than five to ten minutes to read and understand.

When I look at all of these forty strategies pulled together in one place like this, I am forcibly struck by an important insight — I have learned all of what I've written about here from the endless procession of infinitely more talented people I've had the privilege of working with over my years in business. I've learned from them, and they have learned from me. That group of collaborators now includes you.

I know that, as you read these strategies, you'll likely think, 'I have another way of addressing that challenge', or 'I wish he had provided an approach to dealing with....' Please let me know what else you'd like me to address in the future, and please share your successful strategies with me (deiric@deiricmccann.com). I'm neither too old nor too conceited to believe that I have all of the answers. You see, as I dot the final i's and cross the final t's, I sense that a second edition is inevitable. I feel as if I've merely come to the end of the beginning of a longer-term project. I'm certain that, with your feedback and input, the next edition will be even more powerful.

I wish you all of the success you deserve, and pray that you'll be blessed with the opportunity to work with the same sort of people I have — people who will make your luck and ensure your success in business.

Deiric McCann
September 2003

Strategy 1

Antelope and Chipmunks

Antelope and Chipmunks

Know Your Goals
and Focus Upon Them

Is your life an antelope hunt or a chipmunk chase?

A former world leader is credited with a view of goal-setting from which we can all learn.

He used an analogy wherein he regarded himself as a lion — the head of the pride, no less — and all of the issues he ever faced as either 'antelope' or 'chipmunks'. Even when a lion is dying of hunger, he won't give chase to any of the many smaller animals, like chipmunks, which gambol nearby, offering a quick and easy snack. Why? Because even if he did make the effort and catch one — and there's always an outside chance that he'd fail — it simply wouldn't satisfy him. However, even when weakened by hunger to the extent that he can hardly move, when an antelope shimmers into view miles away across open plains, the sight moves the lion to action. Even so weakened that he knows a failed effort could be the end of him, the lion commits to the hunt. If there's even a slight chance of success, he'll give his all — because success will fill his belly for weeks to come. The greater reward is worth his all, and so he begins the long process of focused effort that he clearly envisages will end in a successful kill.

A single-minded focus upon clearly defined 'antelope' is what also characterises most successful businesspeople.

Have you identified your *antelope*? Do you hunt them every day at the expense of less-satisfying chipmunks? Look out across your plains and spot your own *antelope*.

1. Think about your life or your business and write down what you'd like to achieve. Would you like to drive your company sales up to €10M, write a book, or tramp through the Himalayas? Write down everything you'd ever like to achieve.

2. Take time to identify the one item on your list that, more than any of the others, gets you excited and deep-in-the-gut passionate when you consider achieving it. This is your first antelope — shimmering in the heat of day, miles out on the plain of your life.

> If there's a slight chance of success, the lion commits all.

3. Focus on this first antelope. Build a clear picture of it in your mind. How will you feel when you catch it? How will it change your life? What will your loved ones say? Get a clear mental picture of exactly how the end of that successful hunt will feel. See it in full color, full detail. As you sight your first antelope and begin the process of throwing your whole self into an all-or-nothing hunt, you are going to need the energy to keep you in the hunt — even when things become difficult. That energy is passion. Fuel your passion: review the mental picture you've built, and

write down all of the benefits you'll enjoy once you've run this beauty to ground. Write them all down in detail — the more benefits you write down, the greater the passion you'll bring to the hunt.

4. If it were easy to catch antelope, we'd all dine on venison daily! It's not. Write down everything you can speculate might stop you bringing your antelope down, and work out precisely how you'll deal with each of these obstacles. Have a clear strategy to deal with all of those pitfalls that you can predict in advance — it will enhance your confidence and vision.

5. Set yourself clear deadlines. Think about the various stages of a successful hunt. What will you have to do first? How long will it take you to do this (realistically)? When will you be finished with this stage? What has to happen next, and when will that stage be complete? Work your way through all of the stages of a successful hunt. Your target deadline will be the date at which the last stage of your hunt is complete.

6. Now do it again — go back to your list and see if there are any more antelope, and work them down to the deadline stage. Don't separate out a whole herd — simply find one

or two prime candidates. Later, as each is run to ground, you can replace it with a new antelope.

7. Finally, take a 3"x5" card and note all of your antelope as succinctly as you can (including your deadlines). Once they're written, see if you can refine them — make them even sharper and more compelling. Keep this card on you at all times. Read it first thing in the

> *Leave Chip 'n' Dale to those with lesser appetites!*

morning and last thing at night. As you start each day, ensure that you have scheduled some actions that are going to take you closer to your antelope. No day should go by without moving you closer to one or all of them. Don't allow yourself to get distracted by those easier-to-catch chipmunks that present themselves — always keep your focus on those more satisfying meals way out on the plain.

Leave Chip 'n' Dale to those with lesser appetites than yours — get on the trail of your own antelope. Today!

'*Run your day by the clock, but run your life with a vision.*'

ZIG ZIGLAR

Strategy 2

Are You Getting Through?

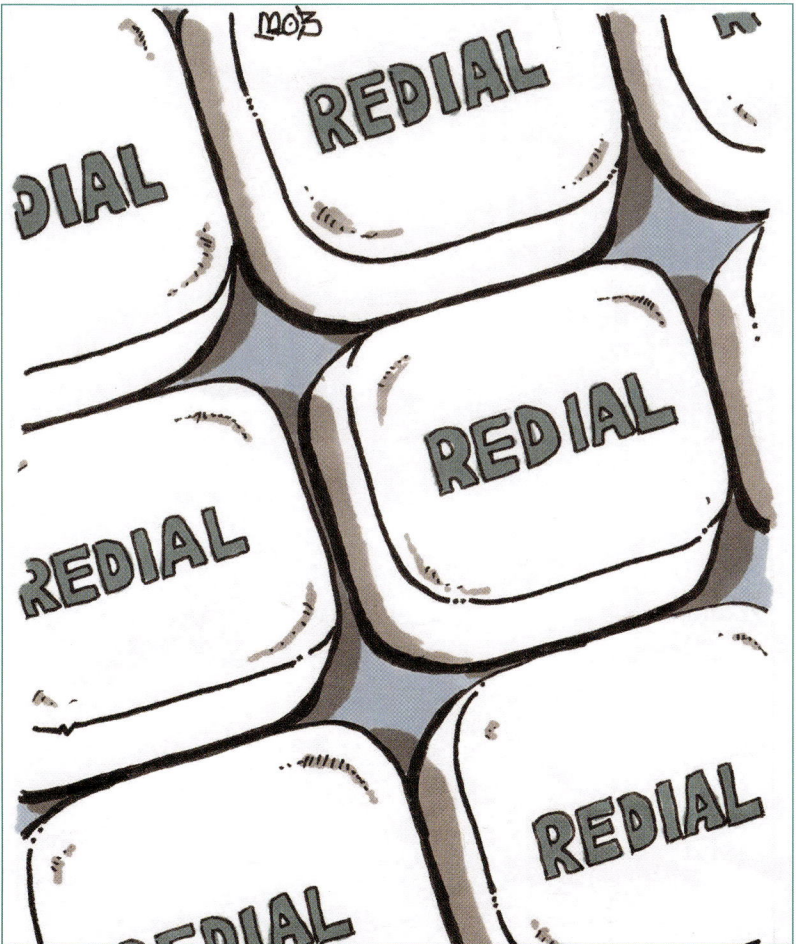

Are You Getting Through?

Making the Telephone
Work for You

Is the success of your organisation dependent upon a constant supply of new clients or customers?

If so, then at the point where the 'rubber meets the road', someone has to make contact with a prospective client for the first time — and this most likely happens by phone. Sure, you or your salespeople may have the courtesy to write to introduce yourself and all of the wonderful things you do, but the real sale starts when you call to follow — to say, *'I'd like to come and see you.'*

Put yourself in the shoes of that prospect for a moment. Do you suppose they're any less busy than you? Ask yourself honestly: do you have time to take calls from people like you or your salespeople? No, I knew you didn't — you're too darned busy. Which is why you and every other prospect in the world start just about every first contact with a potential new supplier (whose call you happened to pick up by accident when the switch had closed for lunch, for example) trying to find reasons to terminate the call and get on with the *really* important business of the day. It's not necessarily a conscious thing — it's just that we all want to get back to our priorities. So, from the moment a call with a prospective new supplier begins, we're all listening for any reasonable opportunity to terminate the conversation.

If this afflicts you or your salespeople, try this imaginative four-step twist on your introductory calls:

First, Greet Them

Manners are manners. Grab their attention with their name — Dale Carnegie rightly said that a person's name is 'the sweetest sound to a person no matter what their language':

> *A person's name is the sweetest sound to them.*

'*Good Morning, Mr Smith…*'

…short, sweet, and to the point.

Second, Tell Them Who You Are, Right? Wrong!

They don't care! They probably haven't heard of you or your company before and, even if they have, it didn't motivate them to seek you out, did it? No — next give them some reason to want to talk with you. Grab their attention and whet their appetites:

> '*I'm calling to tell you how we've helped Money Bank Corporation to cut their staff turnover from 40 per cent to just 10 per cent in under twelve months, and to see how a similar programme might be of interest to you.*'

The key here is research. You've got to know where they are likely to be hurting, what issues are facing this person, precisely how you can help them and, ideally, you will have a

9

quotable example of the sort of results you've achieved for someone just like them — someone they know faces similar challenges.

Only Then Do You Introduce Yourself

Now that you've got their attention and interest, they are more likely to be wondering, 'Who is this?'

> *'My name is Jim Selby, and I'm calling from HR Associates.'*

And Finally, Ask for an Appointment

What you have to relate to them is beyond effective discussion by telephone, so ask to meet them. Keep it succinct:

Four steps:
Greeting
Attention Grabber
Introduction
Appointment

> *'It wouldn't be practical to take you through this detail on the phone. Would you be available during the week of 12 May to meet briefly so I can walk you through how we achieved results for Money Bank, and see if a similar programme might be of benefit to you?'*

Always offer a specific day or week, and allow them to offer an alternative date suited to their commitments.

So, the four steps are:

1. Greeting
2. Attention Grabber
3. Introduction
4. Appointment

This simple formula is time-effective, easy to master and — most importantly — proven in practice.

But what if you don't even get past first base? What if your call is intercepted by the dreaded voice mail? Use the same approach. Think about most of the voice-mail messages you receive from prospective suppliers trying to get your attention. Most of them either have an entirely selfish focus upon what they want: '*My name is … and I need to meet you*', or they adopt the mystery-caller approach: '*My name is Jim Selby. I'll call back later.*' Avoid these ineffective message forms — use the opportunity you have to grab this key prospect's attention. Take the same four-step approach to build a *Killer Voice Message*.

Before you call, rehearse a 30-second pitch that goes all the way from your initial greeting, through the attention grabber, introduction and request for appointment — and don't forget to suggest the week or day that best suits you. Leave your number. And, if you get their voice mail next time, leave your *Killer Voice Message* again, and again.

Leaving this sort of focused and complete information in your voice message provides your prospect with the wherewithal to decide whether or not what you have to say is of sufficient interest for them to meet you. If you construct your message well enough, and if there is good enough reason for them to want to see you, the eventual outcome will be positive — even if they don't rush to the phone the first time they hear your pitch. I've frequently had clients call me back after I've left several *Killer Voice Messages* — to thank me for my persistence, explaining that they were interested from the first time they heard my messages but were too busy to follow up there and then. I've also had people come back and tell me, '*No thanks*' or '*Not now*'. This, too, is positive, saving me from making future calls to them, and allowing me to focus that time and effort where it has more chance of success.

Use this simple proven formula to prepare every appointment call you ever make — ensuring to allow and plan for the possibility of voice mail — and you'll get to more appointments in less time than any other way.

Am I getting through?

Strategy 3

How to Become an Employer of Choice

How to Become
an Employer of Choice

Attracting and Retaining
the Very Best People

Even as we complain about the difficulty of attracting and retaining the sort of people essential to our organisations' success, there are some employers who seem able to do so as easily as they ever did. What's the secret of these 'Employers of Choice'?

It's not really a secret as such — they simply know what's important to their prospective and current employees and they work hard to ensure that they provide it.

Before you can look at the whole area of attracting and retaining people in any realistic manner, you must first look at the dark side — at what drives people from their jobs. Profiles International recently completed a survey on why people leave their jobs. The results were fascinating. The following were the six main reasons cited by the respondents for their job change:

- Bored with the job

- Inadequate salary and benefits

- Limited opportunities for advancement

- No recognition

- Unhappy with management and the way they managed

- Other reasons.

Before I reveal the relative importance of each, give yourself a test. Consider which ones you'd expect would get the largest percentage hit rate. In other words, if you wanted to retain your people, which ones would you address first? When you've thought about it, turn to the insert at the end of this strategy and see how you fared. Then carry on reading the rest of the strategy.

* * *

Welcome back! Were you surprised? Most employers are. The message is simple — if you want to attract and retain your key people, these are the key items for consideration.

Follow these six steps and you too could become an *Employer of Choice*:

Step 1. Look at Your Managers

The numbers don't lie. People leave people, not jobs. Look at the results — 30 per cent of people didn't leave their jobs; they left their managers. Poor managers can completely cancel out the positive effects of your heavy investment in recruitment advertising and PR, in killer remuneration packages, in your outstanding share option scheme, and all of the other good things you do to attract and retain the right people. Your HR people

People leave people, not jobs.

15

sweat blood to bring in a sufficient number of these right people and, in 30 per cent of cases, poor managers shred them and send them back out of the company before you've even recovered the cost of hiring them. Crazy.

So what do you do? First, start measuring your staff turnover by *manager* — find out where the real problems are. It will frighten but enlighten you. Unless you know which managers are losing their people, you can't do anything about it. To help these managers improve their game, you first have to identify them.

Second, review all of your managers in terms of their leadership and management skills. That way you'll find out what exactly is driving your people away. Use Profiles *Multi-Rater Checkpoint* to give each and every manager, their boss, their direct reports, and their fellow managers an opportunity to provide feedback on what they are doing well — and what they could do better. Then, act upon what you discover. Provide training, coaching and support to those managers who struggle to manage their people in a way that encourages productivity and retention.

Good management is key to good retention.

Step 2. Create a Recognition Culture

Insufficient recognition for the contribution they make is why 25 per cent of all people leaving their jobs do so. Fix this or learn to live with the attrition. Task your managers with the responsibility for seeking out the many ways in which their people perform above and beyond the call of duty. Have them consciously seek out opportunities for positive recognition. Institute award schemes for exemplary performance

16

and give everyone an opportunity to bask in the glow of positive recognition for a job well done. But be aware that a recognition culture cannot be created from nothing — it requires a healthy working environment to thrive.

Step 3. Create a Healthy Working Environment

To encourage development of a genuine recognition culture, you'll need to create a healthy working environment. Not healthy in the sense of lots of fresh air and few toxic chemicals knocking around (although that's always a good start), but a healthy *psychological* working environment — one where providing recognition for exemplary performance seems normal.

There are several key elements to achieving this. First: **Open Up Communications**. There are too many old-economy attitudes abroad in our businesses. In the old economy, scarcity was the driving force — information was power, and those who had information hoarded it and kept it scarce. That way, they amassed great power, privilege and wealth. Look around — the world has changed dramatically. Our modern economy is based on abundance — those who prosper are those who share information with everyone and anyone who can make use of it effectively. This is the information age, and any environment where the workforce is not tapped into all that's going on in their organisations is toxic. Suspicion, mistrust and resentment grow — and key people go.

Let all of your people know where the organisation is going; how it plans to get there; how their jobs play a part in the grand scheme of things; and why they are key to your success. Their contribution is just as valuable as the CEO's, and they know it. Let them know that you know it too. Spread information liberally throughout your organisation; give your people an *I'm on the inside!* feeling — it's hard to leave something that has you on the inside.

Next, **Develop an Attitude of Co-operation**. Give and take is the order of the day. Be prepared to consider anything that makes it easier and more practical to work for you than for anyone else. Look at flexible hours, compassionate leave, sabbaticals, teleworking, childcare facilities — anything you can afford to do that shows that you are prepared to meet your people halfway (or more) in balancing their work/personal life commitments.

Finally, **Develop an Atmosphere of Trust**. If you want people to trust you (with their jobs, their careers, their development — their lives), then you have to trust them. Create an atmosphere where management automatically expects the best of its teams — they'll respond. Give people a good reputation to live up to — they won't let you down. This is one of the key sources of recognition — no one is more flattered than when they are trusted implicitly.

Step 4. Create an Atmosphere of Continual Self-Improvement

Of the people who leave their jobs, 20 per cent do so because they feel that they're not getting sufficient advancement to retain them. Not surprising, really. Our new flat-structured organisations don't have the dizzying promotional heights that previous generations of workers could aspire to scaling. So, there's really nothing we can do about this point unless we still have an old-fashioned multi-layer hierarchical organisation, right?

No! That thinking is about as wrong as you can get. Modern job-seekers wants the opportunity to develop themselves *to be all that they possibly can be* — to continually polish their skills, abilities and experience so that their potential market value continually rises. And if they can do this without the uncertainty of job-hopping, then so much the better. So you don't necessarily have to have multiple promotional opportunities to meet this demand. What you need is a clear, ongoing development path — a way that each and every one of your people can advance their skills and value so that they become all that they can be. This means heavy investment in training and development.

Create an atmosphere of continual self-development — give everyone access to any training that will enhance their skills, their value, and their self-esteem. Don't be boxed in to limiting the training available to those skills specific to an individual's current job. Remember that you are not simply training for job-effectiveness but are also offering your people the development opportunities that make

> *Help your people to be all that they possibly can be.*

them feel good enough about the pace of their *personal* advancement that they don't feel the need to seek out greener grass elsewhere. Invest heavily in training and development, and then actively encourage your people to take advantage of your programmes. Provide them with the means for success — train them on company time; give them study leave; have senior managers coach and support them. Engage them in their own ongoing, longer-term development. Show them how they can get all of this development from within your organisation; focus their minds on genuine development goals that extend far beyond the availability of the next recruitment supplement. This creates truly compelling and self-serving reasons to stay.

Well done! If you implement these first four steps, you've already eliminated 75 per cent of the reasons why people leave their jobs, and we haven't even mentioned money yet!

Step 5. Put Your Best Foot Forward

What about the 15 per cent who leave for more money? Will more recognition, better management, and opportunities for continual self-development retain them? In many cases, yes (at least for a time). Sadly, however, you still have to pay the market rate or better to stay in the game. But when and how you pay this level is key.

As you read this strategy, chances are that you're sitting down. Good. Because the next suggestion can topple some old-style thinkers. When it comes to remuneration, put your best foot forward immediately. Pay your people as much salary, give them as many benefits as you can afford — and do it from day one.

Abandon the '*What can I get her for?*' thinking in favour of '*How much is this position worth to me, and what can I afford to pay?*' Then pay it. Let your people know that this is what you're doing, and that you need their support and effort to help you to maintain a situation where you can continue to do this in the long term — that you need them to engage with you in making the organisation successful.

Think about it sensibly — if you pare back the package at offer time by the 10 or 15 per cent you can get away with, will this 10/15 per cent be enough to retain these people in the face of an offer from another employer? Most likely not — it will be too little, too late. So, put your best foot forward — and let them know. Let everyone know that you are paying absolutely as much as you can and that, for you to continue to do so, everyone will have to pull together as a team to generate the productivity necessary for the organisation's success. We all respond to fair treatment.

Now, don't misunderstand the advice — pay as much as you can, not more than you can. Pay more than you can afford and you'll just become employer road-kill. Know what each job is worth, and pay it early.

Step 6. Match People to Jobs

Having followed 360,000 people through their careers over a twenty-year period, a major study by *Harvard Business Review* demonstrated that a key ingredient in retaining people is ensuring that they are matched to their jobs in terms of their abilities, interests, and personalities. The study found that when you put people in jobs where the demands of the job matched their own abilities, where the stimulation offered by the job matched their particular interests, and where the cultural demands of the position matched their personalities, staff turnover went down dramatically, and productivity went up dramatically.

Use psychometric tools to determine the requirements of each of your positions in terms of abilities, interests and personality, and then use this information to match your jobs to people who will excel in them. Gut feeling cannot do this assessment for you — it needs to be undertaken using properly validated tools designed for this purpose. (You can find more information on *The Profile*, a business tool designed to make job matching easy, at:

www.profilesinternational.com)

Once you know what each job requires, you can more effectively match people to their jobs, providing any training, support, or coaching necessary for them to be successful. Put the right person in the right job and you eliminate a large portion of the 5 per cent who leave simply because they are 'bored with the job'.

Sadly, there is no quick, easy and inexpensive 'silver bullet' that will help you to win the war for quality people. But apply these six sensible steps and you eliminate over 95 per cent of the reasons why people defect — putting yourself well on track to be one of that envied class — the *Employer of Choice*.

How Did You Do?

The study found that of the job-leavers surveyed:

- 30% were unhappy with management and how the management team managed.

- 25% felt that they got no recognition for good work.

- 20% complained of limited opportunities for advancement.

- 15% cited inadequate salary and benefits. (Low, isn't it?)

- 5% were bored with the job.

- 5% cited other reasons (retirement, career change, sabbatical, travel).

So, if you want to attract and retain the people essential to your success, these are the key factors that you have to consider — and the priorities are abundantly clear. Money, for example, is important — but not nearly as important as most employers seem to believe.

Return to where you were in the strategy to see what you can do to make practical use of this insight.

'There is nothing more important to your success than hiring great people. Nothing.'

LOU ADLER

HIRE WITH YOUR HEAD

Strategy 4

Big Dogs Expect to Win

Big Dogs Expect to Win

Fake it Till You Make it!

When a big dog comes on the canine scene, all of the others sit up and take notice. If there's going to be a scrap, they all know that the big dog is likely to win. But sometimes you see a fierce mini-pooch get into a dog fight and wipe out all of the competition — that's because the mini-pooch knows the *Big Dog Code*, and follows it.

Whether your company is a poodle or a Rottweiler, when you follow the *Big Dog Code*, you'll find that you expect to win too. Here are the bones of the *Big Dog Code*.

Big Dogs Bay the Moon

A full moon is the best promotional opportunity in the *Big Dog* calendar, and no pooch worth its bones misses the opportunity to let loose and let everyone know it's around. *Big Dogs* bark first, bark loudest, and keep right on barking long after all of the lesser mutts have abandoned the opportunity. Seek out as many platforms as you can to howl out the many reasons why your potential customers should sit up and take notice. There are lots of them and, like the moon, many can come to you for free. Seek out speaking engagements at key industry events, and host or sponsor useful seminars for the industry associations involved in your marketplace. Look, also, for opportunities to contribute articles on your areas of expertise to industry journals. When the *Big Dog* starts baying the moon, all of the rest of the pack joins in eventually — but all that anyone remembers is the one who barks first, barks loudest, and barks consistently.

Big Dogs Don't Chase Cars

Big Dogs don't waste their time chasing cars — they leave that to the mutts. They know that even if they caught the car, they wouldn't know what to do with it. You can't eat it! Focus your efforts on chasing only opportunities where, when you've run them to ground, you get some worthwhile return for your efforts. Before you start chasing prospects, be sure that you know what you're going to do with them when you catch them, and be sure it's worth the effort. Chase only prospects who have adequate need for your products, have the wherewithal to pay for them, and have a credit record that suggests they will, and are likely to, yield some kind of profit. Don't get into the habit of chasing anything that moves. Leave that to the mutts. Be cool — you can afford to be selective — you're a *Big Dog*.

Big Dogs Will Hound You until They Get What They Want

If a big dog sees a rival with a bone he fancies, he immediately goes after it — and nothing will stop him until it's his. Even if he's greeted with a snarl and a show of teeth, he'll still simply withdraw a little, recompose himself and come back — again and again.

Research shows that most big deals close after seven client interactions, or more; the same research shows that most salespeople give up after a single 'No!' Winning the best deals takes persistence. Be a *Big Dog* — persist until you get the deals that you want.

Big Dogs Get to Know the Pack

Big Dogs get to know more of the members of their own pack, and of the other packs running in their area. A great benefit of all this sniffing around is that the *Big Dog* is the first to know if someone new is on their patch. This kind of fearless networking is key to looking like a *Big Dog*. Get out and about. Make sure that you meet the maximum possible number of people in your area who might eventually be interested in what you have to offer. Find out who else is operating

> *Fearless networking is a trademark of the Big Dog.*

in your area. Get your nose right into their business and get to know what they're all about. The *Big Dog* knows everyone on his block — friend or foe. Network constantly.

There's No Mistaking a *Big Dog*'s Territory

Once every mega-mutt has successfully seen the competitors off their territory the first thing they do is to mark it. Everything on the new territory is marked with the *Big Dog*'s brand — sending out a pungent 'Keep off! This is mine' message to any potential interlopers. Protect your own territory. Once you've won customers, work hard to keep them. Let them know how much you value them. Find out what it will take to keep them

> Big Dogs *get to know everyone in the pack.*

with you, and work hard with them to deliver it. Then, let the world know — here are my customers; here's why they're anxious to stay with me; and here's why you should be talking with me too. Good relationship management like this will serve to keep other mutts off your patch, and communication of testimonials and successful references will build your *Big Dog* reputation and help to bring in new clients. Once you win some territory, make sure that everyone knows it's yours, and work hard to keep it.

Size Doesn't Matter if You've Got the Pedigree

When you're in a situation where everyone knows that you're not quite as big a dog as you'd like to have them believe, remember a key rule — size doesn't matter if you've

got the pedigree. Act like a thoroughbred. Be totally professional, adhering to a strict code of business ethics, and
looking after the important little details. That way you'll
always get the *Big Dog* respect you deserve. Professionalism
and ethics are key.

Follow the *Big Dog Code*, and everyone will assume that
you're a big dog. Do it — you know you deserve to win!

Strategy 5

Of Course
I Remember You!

Of Course
I Remember You!

Nothing is More Important
to People than Their Names

*'Hey Deiric, let me introduce you to someone I've just met —
this is…er…, er…, I'm sorry, what did you say your name
was again?'*

You're introduced to someone new and, just seconds
later, you can't remember his name when it comes to introduce him to someone else. Or someone walks up to you and
a friend in the street, addresses you by name, and, because
you've no idea of her name, you have to resort to not intro-
ducing her and to constructing a conversation that never
veers close to mentioning her name? Embarrassing? No,
that's too small a word!

Take heart! Unless you're one of a small number of
people worldwide suffering from prosopagnosia — a complete inability to recognise faces, or *face blindness*, if you'd
prefer — then the following steps will save you the embar-
rassment of ever forgetting anyone's name again.

Step 1. Switch Off the Internal Dialogue

As you're reading this strategy, take a moment to examine what else is flying around in your mind — lots of things, right? It's no different in social or business situations where you're meeting people for the first time. Instead of focusing solely on the person you're meeting, your mind is filled with snatches of other concerns flying through it — '...*mmm, he looks nice ... I wonder what that itch is ... when she's finished speaking, I'm going to say ... wow! look at the size of that mole on that guy's....*' With all of that internal dialogue going on, it should come as no surprise that you find your-self embarrassed to have 'forgotten' someone's name — because in reality you just didn't bother to try to remember it in the first place. Become conscious of your internal dia-logue and make a conscious effort to focus your attention exclusive-ly on the external dialogue. Every time you find yourself drifting inwards, step out. Stay external — prepare to remember.

Listen! Good listeners rarely forget names.

Step 2. Listen

Hey, come back! Just because I'm repeating Rule number 1 of good communication — a rule you've had hurled at you time after time — don't ignore this key element. Good listeners rarely forget names. Learn to listen actively; and to do so, apply the next few steps which focus your active listening engine. Focus, and when a new person's name is introduced into the conversation, be sure to hear it!

Step 3. Bury the New Name in Your Memory

First, repeat it in a sentence. Plain and simple everyday courtesy phrases like, '*It's a pleasure to meet you, **Marie***' will do it. This has two effects: firstly, it puts the name immediately into your short-term memory; secondly, it makes the new person feel good — most people love the sound of their own name. If it's an unusual name, ask her to spell it — '*...is that N-I-L-G-U-N...?*' This implants it even deeper in your memory and builds further rapport. Finally, think about the name itself — does it sound like anything else? Is there any way you can make a memorable association? Names like Wood, Holly, Marsh, Guinness, Bush or Green are made for memorable associations. If there's no obvious association, then consider what their names sounds like: McCann (My Can), Harrison (Hairy Son), Kendall (Candle). The process of trying to make these connections helps to bury names further in your memory.

Step 4. Make Eye Contact

When meeting someone, really look at them — make eye contact and smile. Imagine that the name of your new acquaintance is written in big luminous letters across her forehead. Then observe: What makes her face interesting and different? Has she a parting in her hair, or a gap in her teeth? Eyebrows that meet? A long nose? You don't have to stare them out to do this effectively. All of this can be picked up in a few quick glances — if you're prepared to make the effort.

5. Bring it All Together

Now, finish the job of remembering them forever. You've got the name, you've got some memorable association, and you've got some distinguishing physical features. Now, construct a *mind-picture* for this person. Connect their unique physical features with their name's associ- ation to create a picture that will pop into your mind next time you meet them. The sillier the picture, the better.

Construct mind-pictures to remember people's names.

This is an absolutely infallible system — apply it and you'll never forget someone again, although you do need to be sure that your mind-picture is pretty unambiguous.

With a little practice, this process becomes so automatic and instantaneous that you'll find a mind-picture pops into your head pretty much instantaneously for every new person you meet — ensuring that every new face and name is filed away in your mental Rolodex. Forever.

Now ... what did you say your name was again?

35

'Remember that a person's name is to that person the sweetest and most important sound in any language.'

DALE CARNEGIE
HOW TO WIN FRIENDS AND INFLUENCE PEOPLE

36

Strategy 6

Where Does it Hurt?

Where Does it Hurt?

No Pain — No Gain

When you have a problem with your health, or when you simply don't feel well, you visit your doctor. You're typically asked questions like: 'Where does it hurt?', 'What's the pain like?' and 'When did you first notice it?' The doctor doesn't necessarily expect you to know exactly what's wrong with you or how you might be cured.

Your doctor begins by examining your symptoms — your 'pains', if you will — and when you have provided as complete a picture of all of your pains as you can, the doctor has a basis to diagnose the problem. Very often, your actual pains won't directly suggest what is ultimately identified as your ailment. Equally often, the remedy prescribed won't be anything like what you might have expected (think of acupuncture!)

So, what of your clients and their business requirements? Surely they come to you for help with their business 'pains' because they view you in the same light as their doctor — an expert who specialises in helping people like them to solve their sorts of problems. So, it's hardly reasonable to expect them to have fully diagnosed themselves before they turn up at your 'surgery'. And, if they have diagnosed themselves, surely your consultant's oath requires that you investigate their 'pains' to the maximum extent possible before fully accepting their diagnosis. You're the doctor — the expert — after all.

However, while what your client experiences as 'pains' may be very real, they are not necessarily descriptions of their requirements; they are merely clues to them — clues that you must collect, examine and diagnose. And, having diagnosed the cause of these 'pains', you can then suggest the best course of treatment.

> Don't expect your 'patients' to have diagnosed their problems.

In the end, analysing your client's requirements, developing a clear, comprehensive picture of the problem your client is trying to solve, is the most important part of your sales cycle. If you get the requirement wrong, you'll get the solution wrong (and if you're still selling product, and not solutions to client problems, then someone is going to steal away your business over time). If you can't make clients believe that you understand their problem or requirement, you definitely won't convince them that your solution is superior to those offered by all other bidders — because it likely won't be.

'Doctor Knows Best'

So, when preparing to sell to a client, emulate your good doctor's approach:

First, Question the Problem They're Trying to Solve

Working with your team, list the Pains you feel your client is exhibiting. Draw inspiration for this analysis from your experience of the client's industry, from experience with the client themselves, or with their competitors. Speculate on other linked requirements which your research into the client's industry suggests may be issues which the client should be seeking to address, whether or not the client recognises them.

Think: Commercial, Technical and Personal Pains

Commercial Pains are those associated with the general objectives for most good business decisions: *To increase sales; To decrease costs; To improve market positioning.* Ask yourself: 'What do they wish to achieve by solving this problem?' 'Why try to solve it now — what benefits will accrue?' 'What happens if it's not solved?' 'Why have they invited you to help solve it?' 'Have their competitors solved this problem? How?'

> Look for Commercial Pains, Technical Pains, and Personal Pains.

Technical Pains are those that are seen in your client's aspirations to improve some technical process which is key to the health of their business. For example: Do they need to increase production line efficiency? Are line-machinery downtimes a real concern in their industry? Are their current systems unreliable? Would faster, more modern systems improve their bottom line?

40

Finally, as all client organisations are run by people, you must consider the impact that their personal views and objectives have on the way any of their requirements are defined — don't forget **Personal Pains**. Anything you know of the dynamics of the politics in your evaluator group, or in your client organisation as a whole, should be noted as a

Be sure to diagnose the root cause of the pains before you prescribe a cure.

'requirement' — in the sense that these points must also be adequately addressed by your proposal. These personal factors may not be overtly stated, and you probably won't overtly address them, but be sure to recognise them — you must take account of them.

Then, Confirm and Diagnose

Assemble the disparate list of Pains into a number of groups of related Pains — groups to which you can give titles with which your client will feel comfortable — for example, 'Price Performance', or 'Improved Throughput'.

Take this summary to your client and confirm that it is an accurate assessment of their problem. Having discussed your assessment with your client, modify it as required.

41

Now, Cure Them

Now, with a first-class description of your client problem in hand, you are ready to begin to build your solution to that problem.

Follow this approach to identifying client problems, and then build all of your solutions to cure each of the Pains you identify — at the very least, you can be sure that every business proposal you write will get the consideration it deserves.

Remember, Doc — no pains, no gain.

Strategy 7

First Impressions Last

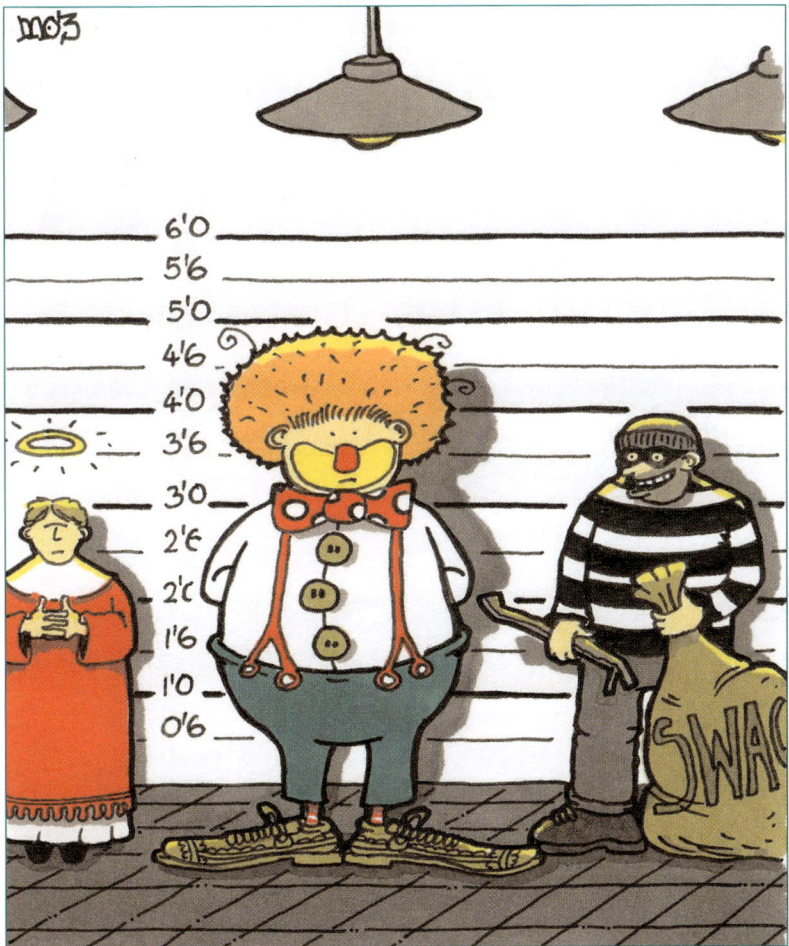

First Impressions Last

Your Image is You

You don't get a second chance to make a first impression. Your company image is all about lasting impressions — so getting your image right is one of the most important exercises you will undertake in assuring the success of your business.

Most people think that their company's image is something that is largely outside their control. It's not. Follow the three steps below to build yourself an image that will foster your business's success.

Step 1. Identify the Image You Want to Project

Before you can build an image, you need to decide what sort of image you want for your business. Ask yourself three questions:

What Sort of Image Should My Business Project?

If you were a banking institution, then you'd be seeking to project conservatism, low-risk and good standing. If, on the other hand, you were a Silicon Valley electronics company, you'd want to project an image of innovation, pioneering, risk-taking and so on. Even your family postman's success depends on projecting an image — of utter reliability. Decide whether you want your customers to view you as innovative, reliable, conservative, bold, progressive, traditional, professional, friendly, etc. — come up with one or two words that effectively capture the image you'd like to project.

Your image should spring from what your target customers expect.

Who are My Target Customers?

Whatever else you do, you must ensure that your image closely matches the image that your target customers have of themselves. Who are your target customers? Where do they currently go for advice on products and services like yours? How much do they have to spend? If you were a hotelier, you wouldn't establish a luxury Park Lane hotel in a low-income area. There's simply no point in being the most expensive or best of class in your area if nobody in your area can afford to shop with you. Equally, you'd be squandering the potential (and the likely higher property costs) in a high-income area by establishing a budget hostel. For optimum success, be sure that there are enough of the sort of customers you'd like to target to make the business work, and that the image you decide to project matches your target customers closely enough to attract them to you.

45

Who is My Competition?

Look at the image of your most successful competitors. If you have an outstandingly successful competitor, you'll want to figure what aspect of the image they project fosters this success. Are they very reliable? Have they a strong service orientation? Have they an incredibly wide range? You'll want to adopt those elements of their image that are positive, and enhance them with whatever you feel makes your business special. If your closest competitor's primary image is based upon their offering an extraordinarily wide range, you'll want to adopt this aspect of their image and enhance it with, say, your reputation for extremely friendly service and high levels of customer attention. Don't try to compete with successful competitors' images head on — assimilate them and improve upon them.

Step 2. Build an Identity that Projects Your Desired Image

So, now you know what sort of image you'd like to project. It's time to build a vehicle — an identity — which will allow you to project that new image effectively.

Start with a Logo

A good identity is about consistency. All of the ways in which you communicate with your customers must have a consistent and considered look and feel. That look and feel begins with a good logo. There are many other aspects to a company identity, but few are more important than your logo. When it appears over your door, on your business card, on your letterhead, in advertisements, and on brochures, your logo should instantly convey your desired image. For this reason, design of a logo is not for the layman. Get professional help. There is a myth that designers are very expensive to work with — this needn't be so. Besides large graphic-design studios that might cost a little more, there are many freelance graphic designers who will work with you to help you to craft a logo that works well for you. You'll find plenty in the Golden Pages. Don't skimp on your logo — in the long run, poor communication of your image will cost you more than a designer ever will.

> *Don't skimp on getting your image right — it's false economy.*

Working with Designers

Designers are like solicitors and other professionals — they work better when you have a good brief for them to follow. So, before you sit down with your designer, do some thinking about the basics of your required logo. Doing so will save your designer time, and thereby save you money.

The main elements you need to think about are:

- **Taglines**

  Taglines are the five- or six-word slogans that often accompany a logo. We all know that '*Pepsi Cola Hits the Spot*', and that Avis rent-a-car will tell you, '*We try harder*'. These one-liners are intended to enhance the message portrayed by the logo, and to make it more memorable. Developing a one-liner like this BEFORE meeting with your designer can make their job a lot easier.

Think of the main aspect of the image you wish to convey which you feel sets your business apart from that of your competitors, and will appeal most to your customers. If you emphasise the family in your business, then your tagline might be something like: 'Not just a garden centre — a family centre'. Build a six- or seven-word one-liner around whatever is the key aspect of the image you want to foster. If you have a tagline in place, the designer knows precisely what image their creation must project for you.

- **Colour**

Colour is an important part of the image your logo will communicate. Reds, yellows, oranges and other bright colours tend to suggest pioneering, trendsetting and fun; whilst colours like blue, grey and darker greens tend to suggest a quieter, more mature and conservative image. Look at the dominant colours in bank logos — they say it all. What colours are appropriate to the image you've selected? Be careful not to be swayed by colours that you might like personally but that might be at odds with your intended image. A good way to begin is by thinking carefully about the sort of colours you certainly *don't* want to use — this will be of great help to your designer.

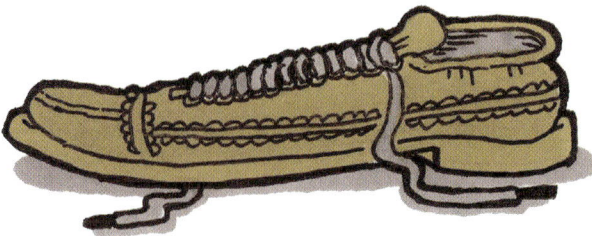

● Typefaces

The image conveyed by the more formal typefaces used in newspapers is vastly different from that projected by simple handwriting typefaces, which is, in turn, different from the image portrayed by heavily stylised modern alphabets. The typeface you choose is one of the strongest image cues your logo can provide. If you know what sort of image you want to project, your designer will be able to advise on appropriate typefaces.

● Graphics

You will find that designers are very adept at producing clever graphical representations of the message that you want to convey. If you do decide to use a graphic element in your logo, be sure that it is easy to understand, and that *the logo still communicates your message even if a potential customer doesn't 'get' the point of your graphic.* In other words, use graphics to enhance a logo that uses words to convey your image — don't let the graphic dominate. It could confuse and project the wrong image.

3. Now You've Got Your Identity — Use it to Project Your Image

It's time to start using your new identity to build your image.

Use Your Logo Everywhere

Your logo is at the heart of your company's identity, and it will successfully communicate your desired image only if you use it effectively. Your logo must appear on all signage, vehicles, letterheads, invoices, business cards, envelopes, packaging, staff uniforms and overalls — on anything that issues forth from your company. Look for all opportunities to use your logo in everyday situations. For example, there are many inexpensive, easy-to-use graphics programs that allow you to produce first-class p-o-s materials with little effort or fuss. Use them.

You should also integrate your logo colours, typefaces and graphics into other less obvious parts of the business. If your main logo colour is blue, then your staff uniforms, vehicles, and even internal furnishing and decorating schemes should also be blue. Effectively projecting your image is all about using absolutely every opportunity to put all aspects of that image in front of your target customers.

It's key that your team understands the image you need to project.

Be Sure that Your Employees Buy Into the Image

A key to projecting a consistent image to your customers is ensuring that the members of your employee team understand the image you are trying to project, what values it encompasses, and how that translates into everything they do. This needs to be integrated into every aspect of your business — from the way you answer the telephone to the way you deal with customers on a day-to-day basis. Take the example above of the centre that is trying to differentiate its image on the basis that it is family-friendly. A chirpy '*Good morning. McCann's family garden centre — how may I help you?'* would project the desired image much more effectively than a simple 'Hello!' The centre would also need to extend this image down to the shop floor — ensuring that the staff and facilities were child-friendly. There would be family-oriented facilities like a baby-changing room, and kids' books and toys would be available; even the décor of the premises would project the centre's focus upon the family. The centre would prove its commitment to its image in everything it does.

Successful images are built upon repetition of the image at every opportunity.

'Can I Change My Existing Image?'

Absolutely. If you have an established identity that has failed to build the image you desire to the level you'd like, change it. You may be concerned that some elements of your existing identity are successful in their own right, and still relevant. For example, your logo may already be quite well known, even if it's not quite conveying precisely the image you'd like. Work out which parts of your current identity you'd like to retain, and then go through the exercise of creating your identity in the manner discussed above. When it comes to logo redesign, you'll find that working with your designer to come up with a new logo that fits your new idea of the identity you require, but still retains the better elements of your previous identity, is a lot easier than you might have expected.

Your company image is something that you need to review regularly as your business grows and expands, and your target customers mature or change. Take a look at your image on a regular basis. Is the image you're projecting still what you need? Is the identity that got you to where you are now appropriate to your development over the next few years? If not, fine-tune it.

The image of your business is one of your most important assets. The small investment of time, effort and money you make in it now will realise far greater returns long into the future. Invest in your image now and make a lasting impression.

Strategy 8

Fire 'em Up!

Fire 'em Up!

21 Days to a Winning, Motivated Team

Will you give ten minutes each day for the next 21 days to fire your team up like never before?

Here's a distillation of all you need to know to motivate people — it's drawn from all of the great writers on the subject — along with a simple 21-day plan for getting all of your team fired up.

Employees Want Management They Can Look Up to — Not Management that Looks Down on Them

An honest respect for all, a genuine recognition that everyone has something good to offer — this is at the heart of the successful motivator. Without respect, so-called motivation becomes manipulation — and manipulation is never successful in the long term. If you or your managers cannot show respect for your people, then, before you invest time and energy in motivational efforts, get someone who can — and have them read on from here!

Take an Interest in the Career and Personal Goals, Aspirations, Interests, Lives and Families of Those who Work with You

No one cares how much you know until they know how much you care — about them! 'Motivation' is about giving your people a '***Motiv***e for ac***tion***'. Understand what your people value and you can more easily formulate a way in which doing what you need them to do will help fulfil not just your goals, but theirs. Take an honest interest in every one of your people and the means to motivate them will become readily apparent. Make it a goal to learn something new about at least one of your people — every day.

The Best Way to Knock a Chip off a Person's Shoulder...

...is to let them take a bow! Do you know anyone who complains about getting too much recognition or praise for a job well done? Do you? Yet, research consistently shows that people will go to extraordinary lengths for a leader who takes the time to catch them doing something right and, when they do, provides them with sincere praise and recognition in front of their colleagues. Praise and recognition are more motivating than money or any other single thing we can give to the people we lead.

> The best way to knock a chip from a person's shoulder is to let them take a bow.

Don't Criticise, Condemn or Complain

Dale Carnegie nailed it with this gem. When you must draw attention to poor performance, don't criticise — coach. Don't pick upon what is being done wrong, but focus all of your attention on the new behaviour or action that will put things right; and always finish with a positive comment that lets them see that the reason you've raised the matter is that

55

you have seen that they are capable of so much more. Correct the errant action, provide some positive feedback, and then forget it. Act like you expect better performance next time — and you'll get it.

Request — Don't Order
Real leaders lead from the front — they don't need to push from the back. Everyone rebels to some extent against being 'bossed around'. No one minds being asked to help.

Discuss — Don't Argue
Maturity is being able to disagree agreeably.

Be Careful with Humour
Avoid any kind of demeaning humour. If there's the slightest chance of being misunderstood, keep it to yourself. 'If in doubt, leave it out.'

Listening is the Greatest Compliment...
...you can pay anyone — our opinions are all sacred to us. Listen — and hear your people's concerns.

Most Importantly of All...
Model the behaviours, attitudes and morale level you expect others to display — show them it works.

21-Day Action Plan
Why 21 days? Well, that's what research shows it takes to establish a habit. Take the motivators discussed above and apply them for 21 days. What you'll find is that by the end of this 21-day period, you will be doing all of these things naturally. And the level of motivation in your team in general —

even in your 'toughest cases' — will be at an all-time high. To implement your plan:

1. *Create a table* with each of your team names down the left-hand side, and each of these motivators across the top. Rule your table so that each person has a box against each motivator.

2. *Target improvements.* Copy this strategy and put it in a place where you can review it at the start of each day. Each day, determine that you will apply each motivator as often as possible with as many members of your team as you can. Plan to speak to each of your team-members often enough that you get to know what turns them on and off; determine to catch them doing something right; praise them in front of their colleagues; listen to their opinions, and so on. At the end of each day, put a tick in your table for each motivator you effectively applied with each team-member. Make sure that your table is filling evenly with ticks — that all motivators are being applied across the whole team. Be careful not to fall into the trap of simply working with those you already get along with, those you like, those who are in least need of some real motivational lift, or with the motivators that come most naturally to you.

3. *Review and Repeat.* At the end of your first 21-day period, stand back and admire the difference you'll have made. Pat yourself on the back, and start all over again. Select

the next person you need to target specifically, and start a new table for the team at large.

Motivation is easy — if you care enough to put in a little extra effort. Anyone can motivate, and anyone can be motivated. All it takes is the right person in the right place, managed by someone who cares. Invest a little of your time over the next 21 days and fire 'em up like never before.

Strategy 9

Talk 'em Down!

Talk 'em Down!

Make Customer Complaints Work for You

No matter how good you, your products/services and your people are, you will occasionally encounter an angry customer. A normally reasonable, happy customer transforms into a flesh-eating beast, bent on your destruction, and comes at you foaming at the mouth and demanding satisfaction. How do you talk 'em down from the ceiling?

There are two traditional ways. The first is to eat crow immediately, accepting the blame fully, begging forgiveness, kissing up, and doing everything the customer asks in order to satisfy them. That way you'll likely keep the customer — but once you've crawled like that, can you look at yourself in the mirror? Probably not. Another approach is to become angry back at the customer, slugging it out with them, exchanging blame and insults, denying all responsibility and telling them where to get off. That way you needn't worry about repeat complaints. After all — no customers, no complaints.

Calming an angry customer and resolving a complaint to their complete satisfaction need not mean sacrificing your self-respect. Apply the following guidelines and I promise you that you'll resolve more problems more easily, turn a complaint into a more positive experience for the customer, and still be able to look at yourself in the mirror.

1. It's Your Problem, But Don't Take it Personally

It may not be your fault, but it's still your problem. Approach all angry customers with this attitude. Even if it is your fault, don't take the complaint personally. Customers complain because they want you to address a perceived shortcoming — not because they don't like you. Resist the temptation to fight back — even if you win the battle, you'll lose the war. And the customer.

> *It may not be your fault — but it's still your problem.*

2. Listen

In order to address the customer's problem, you'll need to know exactly what the problem is. As with all other endeavours, listening is a key skill. Shut up and listen carefully. Besides giving you some insight into the reason for the customer's distress, it also helps to exorcise some of the initial anger the customer is feeling.

3. Don't Interrupt

Let complainants express themselves — don't stop them mid-flow. Let them vent their anger; it will be easier to reason with them afterwards.

4. Calm Your Complainant and Clarify the Problem

When your customer has finished, show some empathy — explain that you understand why they're so upset and that you're going to try to sort things out. Then clarify your understanding of their problem. Ask questions, qualify comments. This will calm them and ensure that your suggested solution will address all aspects of the perceived problem. Step into your customer's shoes. Look at your company, your products, their problem and your actions from their perspective — and then decide whether or not their complaint is justified.

5. If it's Your Fault, Say So. If it's Not, Don't

When you fully understand the complaint, decide whether or not your company is at fault. Don't automatically accept blame before you know that it's warranted. But if it is clearly your fault, admit it early in the process. Accept responsibility and don't hide; don't try to pass the buck. Adopt a genuinely humble tone.

6. Solve the Problem

Think about how best to solve the customer's problem. If you need some time to come up with a response, tell them so and commit to getting back to them in a specified timescale — and do so. Make sure that all of your responses project a clearly concerned but calm manner. Stress your eagerness that the problem be resolved, and project a calm confidence that you are the person to do it. When you have a suggested solution, agree with the customer the steps you'll take and the timescale. Assure them that you'll take personal responsibility for seeing the resolution through — and do. Nothing is more important than resolving customer complaints — attend to them with the utmost urgency. Research shows that it costs at least ten times more to recruit new customers than to retain existing ones.

7. Don't Accept Abuse

Don't accept it if a complainant steps over that almost invisible line between the reasonable right to complain and outright personal abuse. Calmly explain that you are going to endeavour to address any problems they may have, but that you can do that only if they accord you the courtesy and respect you intend to accord them. If they continue with their abuse, terminate the conversation.

8. Pin Down Moving Targets

If you're dealing with a problem that seems to grow every time you implement an agreed solution, ask your customer to put their complaint down in writing so that you can better understand and address it. This will help you to focus upon an agreed solution. Also, working things out on paper can sometimes make a complainant recognise if theirs is an unreasonable viewpoint.

9. Stop it from Happening Again

Try to prevent angering customers in the future:

- At purchase time, let your customers know that it is your policy to resolve any difficulties they might encounter with their purchase. Then, should they call to complain, their stress levels should be a little lower — given their confidence that they'll receive good support.

- Keep in touch — if something's about to happen that might upset customers, let them know before it's an issue.

- When a customer identifies a problem, change what you do to minimise the chance of the problem recurring.

Customers who take the time to complain are generally telling you that they want to continue doing business with you — but with some changes. Put a high priority on resolving their difficulties — but don't ever feel that you must sacrifice your own self-esteem to do so.

Strategy 10

Customers for Life

Customers for Life

How Much are Your Customers Really Worth to You?

Existing customers are the real assets of any sales-oriented organisation. Knowing their 'Lifetime Value' is key to helping you to make important decisions on how much you can afford to spend on recruiting new customers and, perhaps more importantly, on how best to go about increasing the earnings you achieve from each of these existing customers.

What is 'Lifetime Value'?

The Lifetime Value of a customer is the amount they will contribute to your bottom line over the span of your business relationship with them. Before you can calculate the Lifetime Value of a 'Typical Customer', you need to consider the following:

(a) What's the Value of Your 'Average Sale'?

For this exercise, simply divide your total sales revenue by the total number of sales in your typical year. For the example below, a nominal value of €100 is used.

(b) What's Your Percentage 'Profit Margin'?

The example below assumes a 20 per cent margin.

(c) What's a Typical 'Purchase Frequency'?

You can calculate this by dividing your total number of sales by the total number of customers in a typical year. The example uses a modest three times per year.

> Existing customers are the real assets of a sales-oriented organisation.

(d) What's Your Typical Customer's 'Lifespan'?

How long does your typical customer continue to do business with you? If you're not too sure, then err on the conservative side, using two or three years. The example uses a conservative three years.

(e) How Many 'Referrals' Does Your Typical Customer Give You in a Year?

Referrals are leads which existing clients bring to you. If your customers are happy with the service they get from you, they will often bring you 'referrals'. Most satisfied customers will be pleased to give you referrals — if you ask them for them. Do.

If you ask for them, it would not be unreasonable to expect five referrals a year from an existing client. This is the figure used in the example below.

(f) What's Your 'Referrals Hit Rate'?

How many of these referrals become customers? Given that these leads are pursued on the basis of a known 'recommender', the example uses a hit rate of 40 per cent.

Calculating the Lifetime Value

Armed with this information, you can now calculate your typical client's Lifetime Value.

In order to illustrate the relative impact of the various factors used in calculating this Lifetime Value figure, it is calculated below in five separate steps.

(g) Annual Profit — Typical Customer

(a x b) x (c). In the example: (100 x 20%) x (3) = €60

(h) Lifetime Profit

(g) x (d). In the example: (€60) x (3) = €180

(i) Referrals Value

(e x f) x (h). Successful Referrals become customers, so, in the example, the Referrals Value is:

(5 x 40%) x €180 = €360.

Lifetime Value

(h) + (i). In the example: (€180) + (€360) = €540.

This figure can be quite an eye-opener, and would be even more telling if you factored into your existing accounts the reduced costs of marketing, and the potential for gently increasing your sales to these customers, year after year.

What Use is this Lifetime Value Figure?

The Lifetime Value figure illustrates how important it is to make conscious efforts to retain and develop existing clients. Achieving the same margin through one-hit deals would take 27 new sales! What it also illustrates clearly is how important it is to seek referrals from existing satisfied clients. In the example worked above, the Lifetime Value of the client was increased by a whopping 300 per cent, simply on the basis of referrals that led to new clients.

Additionally, your typical client's Lifetime Value allows you to calculate exactly how much you can afford to spend on winning new clients — before you begin your marketing/sales or account development efforts. In the worked example above, the seller could afford to spend as much as €540 to win a new client, even though the value of a typical sale was only €100, and the margin only €20. This is how book clubs can afford to give you three or four expensive books for 99c the first time you buy from them — they have calculated your expected life-time value.

However, the Lifetime Value figure also points up just how you could dramatically improve the performance of your organisation simply by making small efforts to change any of the key figures used to derive it.

Suppose you made the following modest changes to the example:

- Increase the Average Sale value by 10 per cent;

- Improve the Margin by just 5 per cent — by focusing more on existing accounts where the cost of sale is lower, for example;

- Increase the sales per year by a single sale — stay closer to the account;

- Stretch the Lifespan of the customers to five years — by looking after them better;

- Increase the number of referrals by, say, 40 per cent — two more in the example. If you don't currently chase referrals, this should be easy to achieve;

Calculate it yourself — these modest changes would:

- Increase the annual profit from the typical customer to €110 — a massive rise of almost 55 per cent;

- Increase the profit earned from a typical customer in their lifetime by more than 300 per cent to €550;

- Increase the value of referrals increases to €1,540;

- Increase the Lifetime Value for your typical client to €2,090.

This 387 per cent increase in the Lifetime Value of the typical customer resulted from the cumulative effect of relatively small, and eminently achievable, increases in performance in the accounts.

Lifetime Value is a useful customer barometer. Use it. Put an estimated Lifetime Value on any new client before you pursue them — it will give you a good indication of how much you can afford to spend on winning them. Calculate a Lifetime Value for your existing customers; concentrate on improving the little things in the way you do business with them; and enjoy watching your work pay off in their ever-increasing value to you.

Strategy 11

Dare to be Different

Dare to be Different

Differentiation is Key

Are you a 'me too'?

Do your prospective customers know why they should buy from you rather than from any of your competitors? If your customers can't see any significant difference between you and your competition, the only reliable basis you'll have for winning business consistently is price — and that road leads ultimately to disaster. Selling on price is selling to your competitors' strengths.

Differentiate your offerings using the following four steps.

1. Look at How You Stack Up to Your Competition

What can you do that they can't? What do you do distinctly better? What can they do that you can't? Look at your product or service under five main headings, seeking your particular strengths and your competitors' particular weaknesses.

Price

Are you more or less expensive? Are you considered to be at the top, middle or low end of the spectrum in your market?

Is your pricing policy something that sets you apart from your competitors?

Customer Service

Is there anything about your customer-service approach that is unique? Do you provide more implementation assistance? Better ongoing back-up? Friendlier staff? More attractive terms of service? Better delivery? And so on.

Customers

Who are your best customers currently? Who are the people for whom you can do the best job and still make a respectable margin? Are you best with large, medium or small clients? Do you fare better in long-term relationships or short-term flings? Are you local, national or international (or all three)? Who are your ideal customers?

Product

Are your products or services simply and obviously superior to those of your competitors? Are they faster, more efficient, quieter, easier to understand or use, or quicker to set up? Anything that your product or service offers that is clearly unique will be important to you later. Think about it.

Reputation

What's your brand reputation like? How well known are you? By whom? For what? Who is traditionally attracted to your offerings?

This exercise should ideally involve anyone in your organisation who will have an insight into how you stack up against your competition. Resist the temptation to do it alone — the more minds, the merrier. As you work through the exercise, capture your outcome on paper. For each of the five categories above, capture your analysis on a sheet with two columns — 'strengths' and 'weaknesses'.

The mistake that most people make at this stage is to make a decision to differentiate themselves according to that category in which they are most strongly positioned against their competitors. This is a mistake for it fails to take account of the most important person of all — your customer.

2. Become Your Customer and Think 'WIIFM?'

Do customers or prospects know why they should buy from you rather than from a competitor?

If you fail to consider your customer's perspective, you are doomed to failure from the start. Put yourself in your client's shoes, and ask yourself, 'What is most important and valuable to me when I go out looking for these products and services — What's In It For Me?' Be sure that you have a good feeling for what your customers are REALLY looking for. Find out what they VALUE — in order of importance. Don't assume that you know what your customers want — ask them, and then LISTEN. If they say that they need a good accountant, ask them what, for them, makes the difference between a good accountant and a mediocre one. If they say they want good back-up service, be sure that you understand what makes good back-up service for them.

3. Now Decide How to Differentiate Yourself

Analyse your five sheets. Which category is by far the strongest — the one with the most compelling list of strengths and fewest weaknesses? Which category ranks second, third, and so on? Now, from your research with your customers, which of these categories offer the best VALUE to your customer — which will they be most interested in? There's no point in presenting yourself as the lowest price if your customer's attitude is that price is immaterial — it's quality and service that count; or as offering excellent back-up service if the customer can't afford your price.

You'll know you've been successful when you've identified some categories of strengths that represent areas in which you are truly strong; with attributes that your customer truly values; and uniques that your competition cannot easily copy. Always try to identify more than one category, and rank them in value as differentia- tors. Remember — not everyone will be impressed by the same message.

4. Focus Your Marketing through the Lens of Your Differentiators

You know what sort of messages you need to communicate about your products or services that will ensure that you grab the attention of your target market; you know what messages will most effectively differentiate you from your competitors. Now ensure that these are the only messages communicated by your PR, advertising, sales collateral, your sales force and your support force. Don't confuse your target clients by sending conflicting messages. Continually position yourself as the number one, the expert in your particular sphere of differentiation.

However, be sure to repeat Step 2 on a reasonably regular basis. Customer values evolve, and so must your basis for differentiation. Differentiation is an ongoing process.

Do this and your prospects will know what you do; how what you do is better than what your competitors do; why they should buy from you first; and what's in it for them if they do. This is your competitive advantage.

Dare to be different and you can really start to win business.

Strategy 12

Sizzling Hot Mail

Sizzling Hot Mail

Get Your Prospect's Attention

Most sales letters and mailers go straight to the target reader's trash. How do you prevent your masterpieces from sharing this fate?

Take some direction from AIDA. This classic opera is still the secret to writing sales letters that get results.

AIDA tells you that:

- You've got to grab their **<u>A</u>ttention**

- Then provoke their **<u>I</u>nterest**

- So that they'll **<u>D</u>esire**…

- …taking the **<u>A</u>ction** you want from them

Grab Their <u>A</u>ttention

Most unsolicited mail is opened over the wastepaper bin for faster processing — and unless you've a strategy to break your reader's distraction at this point, all of the wonderful sales copy you sweated over may as well be mailed in your own wastepaper bin — saving you the cost of a stamp.

The best way to get attention is with a large, bold headline. This is the single most important feature of your letter to get right. It can't be rushed. It must be perfect. But what do you put in it? Try one of these five types of leader:

- **Ask a Question** — one that your reader instinctively wants to answer 'Yes!' to.

- **Make a Promise** — *'Reduce your business phone bill by 75% immediately'*.

- **Give Them News** — *'Using AIDA increases sales-letter hit rates by 1000%!'*

- **Tell Them 'How to'** — *'How to have that perfect figure for the beach this summer'*.

- **Provide a Testimonial** — get a client quotation: *'Last year, I couldn't even spell tecknishun and now I am one thanks to Online Learning'*.

Brainstorm with your colleagues and friends to come up with as many possible headlines as you can. Then narrow this list down to the best one by running it past as many people as you can — look for the headline that they think would grab their attention (but don't throw away the rejects — you'll see that you may need them later). When you've got your headline, you're one step closer to more sales: you've got something that will make your prospect read your letter — and that's a pretty good start.

Attention
Interest
Desire
Action

79

Now Get Them Interested

Now that you've got their attention, you've got to describe exactly what it is you can do for your reader. How does your offering work? What does it do? How is it different from others that they might have heard about? Why should they be interested? Outline precisely what benefits the particular features of your product will deliver to them. How could your programme get them in perfect shape in time for summer? How will you '*reduce* [their] *business phone bills by 75%*'? Tell them what you can do for them — and then prove it using compelling examples, testimonials from satisfied customers and successful case histories.

Create a Desire

Now you've got to make them desire what you're offering. This means putting the benefits of your offering in terms that mean something to them personally, that will make them *desire* your offering enough to take the next step with you. Show them how they will feel on the beach if they do have '*the perfect figure for the beach this summer*'. What will they be able to do with the money saved on phone bills? What will it be like to write sales letters that get a ten times better response? How will their new career as a technician change their lifestyles? Use specific datelines and details to make your point: '*...if you start now, by 1 June you could be back in a size ten*'; '*...join our course by January and you could be earning €45K as a technician by year end*'; '*...start* *now and you could double your sale for Q3*'. Make them want you, and then…

Ask Them to Take Action

So what do you want them to do next? Should they phone you? Visit your website? Expect a call? Don't expect your prospect to work it out for themselves — be clear and specific. Tell them how they can act upon the desire you've created. Create a sense of urgency, of '*act now!*' Make it as easy as possible — use mail- or fax-backs, or freephone numbers that they can '*call right now*'. In my own tests, mailers with '*act now*' lines like these outperformed mailer-only shots by more than 20 per cent.

How Long?

There's an old rule of thumb that sales letters should never run to more than one page. It's utter rubbish! Take as much space as you need to paint a clear picture of your offering and of the benefits to your customer of taking it from you — but no more. Don't cripple your pitch by squeezing it into a mean few lines — your headline got your prospect's attention and if your offer is good enough, and you sing AIDA at them, they'll read it

> *Don't cripple your pitch by squeezing it into a mean few lines — take the space you need to paint a clear picture of your offering.*

through. However, don't misunderstand — this is not a licence to ramble on, repeating yourself. When you've said it all, shut up!

If at first…

Don't expect to get it right first time every time. Before you commit to mass mailings, run test batches with a few variations on headlines and content — and fine-tune until you find the one that pulls the maximum response.

P.S.

Always have one — a *p.s.*, that is. People see and take notice of headlines and postscripts. Your *p.s.* is a great opportunity to reiterate why they need to act now — restate your key selling point or benefit or, if you offer a 'no-risk guarantee', get it in here. Give this as much time and consideration as your headline. A good *p.s.* is vital in building real sizzlers.

Think AIDA and sizzling sales letters are just a little hard work away.

Strategy 13

Watch Your Mouth!

Watch Your Mouth!

Be on Your Prospects' Lips

A trusted friend tells you to go and see the latest Tom Cruise movie, that it's your type of story — great acting, a wonderful script, and so on. Chances are that next time you're planning a night at the cinema, you'll take their recommendation — right? Everyone likes the comfort of a recommendation or a testimonial when they're about to invest some time, effort, or money — however small the amount. Word-of-mouth can make or break movies — and just about any other business.

Here's the 'Who?, What? and When?' of good word-of-mouth marketing.

Whose Mouths Can You Enlist?
Friends and Family

There's an unwritten rule that we shouldn't 'mix business with pleasure'. But what if what you have to offer is better than they could possibly get elsewhere? You could be doing your friends and family a favour by giving them the opportunity to do business with you — and once you do a good job for them, they'll want to talk about it.

Existing Clients

If someone continues to do business with you over a long period, it's probably because you're doing something good for them. Remind yourself and them of the value of your relationship, and encourage them to say good things about you to their contacts — and to tell you whom they've said them to!

Prospects

There can be a wide variety of reasons why a prospect is not currently a client — timing, budget, long-term commitments to other suppliers, etc. If your prospects like what you have to offer, seek referrals from them — everyone likes to give their friends help in identifying good suppliers

Everyone likes the comfort of a recommendation when they're about to invest some time, effort or money— however small the amount.

Suppliers

Adopt the attitude that you 'do business with people who do business with you'. OK, so not all of your suppliers will be able or inclined to jump right into a relationship with you, but they should surely be able to help you with some referrals to other customers of theirs who might be able to use your services. Your bank manager and accountant should be good starting points.

Networking Organisations

Networking organisations like Business Network International and Business Link are designed specifically to foster the development of referral networks. In the case of BNI, only one representative from each profession or class of supplier can join a given chapter. They meet weekly to advise their fellow chapter members on how best to sell them into their personal networks. Your local chamber of commerce also probably holds networking events that give you an opportunity to improve your word-of-mouth image. If you don't belong to a networking group, then join one now — otherwise, rest assured that someone else is working your patch.

What Do You Do?

Explain the Value of Referrals to You — and Them

Give examples of referrals where the source of the referral also benefitted from the introduction — by strengthening their ties. Explain that it's only by referrals that your business can prosper and so continue to provide the level of service quality that they and your other clients have come to value.

Use Testimonials

Seek testimonials from satisfied clients — ask them to commit to paper the ways in which your relationship with them has benefitted them or their businesses. Reward this valuable assistance with some additional added value or extra service. Then, when you have these testimonials, use them to establish the credibility, comfort and trust so essential to encourage people to open up their network of contacts to you. Good testimonials will pry open even the most stubborn doors.

Develop a 'Jingle'

Develop a 60-second 'jingle' that outlines what you do, who you do it for, what benefit you bring to your clients, and why it is that you do it better than anyone else. Practise this talk continually until it is brief, snappy, and memorable — and then use it frequently. Repeat it often enough to your contacts and to the people you approach for referrals, and you'll find that your message starts to get about. Even use it when leaving voice-mail messages.

Thank You!

By now it must be standard practice for all effective marketers to send a simple 'thank-you' note to clients every time they do some more business with them. Do the same for those who refer business to you. Let them know how the referral worked out, how you looked after their contact, and how their recommendation has benefitted their contact, them, and you. That way, they'll want to help you again.

Here's a Referral for You!

Who do you know that might be able to use their products and services? 'What goes around, comes around.' Business Karma is one of the most powerful sources of ongoing referral business — 'Givers Gain!'

When Should You Use Word-of-Mouth?

All the time! When you close a sale, ask your new client for the name of anyone else who might have the same problem or challenge that you were able to help them with. Ask for

> *Put your words in as many mouths as possible — and your success will soon be on everyone's lips.*

referrals when you send the thank-you note for new business, or when you make support or service calls. Don't assume that, because you've asked once, your prospect or client is now tuned into your need for referrals — they may have just heard of a need for what you offer but not made the connection because it has been some time since you last reminded them. Even ask when you've finished outlining your products and services to a brand-new prospect (whom you feel has been impressed by what you had to say). Make it a habit to seek referrals continually. Use your jingle.

Happily for those who do recognise the value of word-of-mouth marketing, most businesspeople just don't get it. Take advantage of this opportunity. Put your words in as many mouths as possible, and your success will be on everyone's lips.

Strategy 14

Pass it On

Pass it On

Delegate for Success

If there were a single zero-cost initiative — one that could be implemented immediately, that would motivate your people, improve team morale, grow team skills appreciably, increase productivity and profit, reduce your stress level and free up your time — would you go for it?

There is such an initiative and, by the time you've finished reading this strategy, you'll have a plan in place to implement it for yourself. The *secret* is delegation.

Take out a pen and paper and follow these simple steps to quickly draw up a delegation plan — one that will allow you to maintain effective control of all of your tasks while still delegating effectively.

Look at What You Can Delegate

Recurring or routine tasks are the obvious candidates for delegation. Draw up a list of all tasks you undertake on a regular basis. List them under three columns — 'Task Name', 'Time to Complete', and 'Special Skills?' Mentally work through your week, hour-by-hour, day-by-day. If you need some reminders, pull out your planner or *To Do* list and look for clues there.

Now, review that list for suitability to delegation. Are there any tasks you used to do when you were in a more junior position? (If so, why isn't someone more junior doing them for you?) Which of these tasks could be undertaken by absolutely anyone? Are there any tasks there that require special skills that are in greater abundance in your team than in you? All of these are prospects for delegation. Now, draw a line through anything that is not a suitable candidate for delegation — besides the obvious, these include personal messages (collecting your dry-cleaning), HR issues like reviews or discipline, or management of crises (you're paid to lead). What's left are your *delegables*.

Plan Your Delegation

Draw up a brief description of each *delegable*: why it's undertaken, how it has been done in the past, when it must begin and when it must be completed, and what the outcome of successful completion of the task must be. This last point is key — you must have clear goals for the task, goals that are defined in an absolutely unambiguous manner that will make them easily communicable. What specific results must the delegate achieve in completing the task? You know you have a successful task description if a complete stranger could pick up your description and understand what is required.

Decide whom You Can Delegate to

You can delegate to use an existing team-member's skill more effectively, or to develop new skills in the team. Either match an individual's proven skills to the requirements to

91

the task or match in terms of the particular skill growth that you want to see in any given team-member.

The first thing your delegation candidates will ask (themselves) is *'What's in it for me?'* Identify why the task is important and how it contributes to the overall success of the group — people need to feel that what they are asked to do is truly meaningful. Then, determine what growth or development they will personally achieve from developing competence in completing this new task.

Well done! You now have a delegation plan that you can begin to implement immediately To put it in motion, you'll need to do the following.

Delegate Each Task

Don't do this in a two-minuter over coffee, or as you pass in the corridor. Accord the exercise the time necessary to explain the what, how, where, when and why of the task; what's in it for them; and how and when you will review progress and completion. Take time to *sell* the task and you'll motivate these individuals to successful completion. Demonstrate your confidence in the selected candidates, reassuring them that you will be there as a support should the need arise. If the task is particularly challenging, provide the security of more frequent reviews, with clearly agreed milestones of the progress expected and agreed key points.

> *To delegate successfully, you must have clear goals for delegated tasks.*

92

This is essential to providing you with confidence that you still have control of tasks you've delegated.

Pass Ownership

Accountability without power is de-motivating. Pass the new delegate the necessary authority to complete all aspects of the new task *without* coming back to you. Be clear, however, in setting the upper and lower limits of this authority in a manner that leaves no room for misunderstandings.

Review the Delegation

When you delegate a task, you agree to specific review points. Be sure to undertake these reviews, providing advice and course correction as required. If there are problems, identify the root causes — is it lack of confidence, lack of skills, or something else? Work with the delegate to see how you can jointly address the difficulty. Encourage the delegate to come to you not just with difficulties, but also with their own ideas on how to overcome them. Don't be tempted to review progress more regularly than agreed, or to encourage 'reverse delegation' — where the delegate is at your desk every five minutes asking what to do next.

Celebrate Success

When a delegated task is completed successfully, be sure to recognise the delegate's achievement — provide them with feedback and be sure that their success is known within the group.

93

Do it Again

Every so often, go back and review all of the tasks you're undertaking with a view to pass on as many of those tasks as you can. If you're paid to manage, then manage — don't do.

You don't have to spend money to get greater productivity and profitability, and to improve motivation, reduce your stress level and free up your time — you just have to delegate. Pass it on.

Strategy 15

Getting to Know You

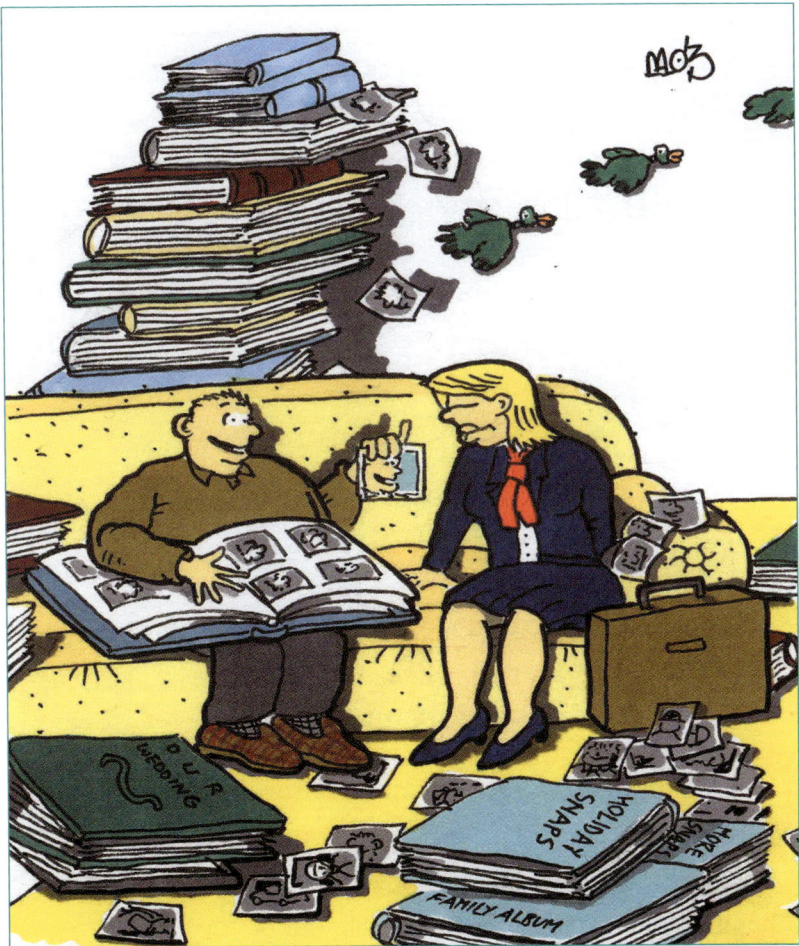

Getting to Know You

Success is All About Relationships

Good products and services, good prices, and excellent after-sales service are no longer any guarantee that your best customers will stay with you forever. A truly loyal customer base can be established only through Customer Relationship Management — the conscious focus of the whole organisation on the development of mutually profitable customer partnerships.

Existing Customers — Your Greatest Assets

There are two ways to increase your sales volume:

- Find new clients;

- Sell more to existing clients by being aware of the range of opportunities that are open to you in every key customer account.

Sales-driven organisations more naturally focus on the first option when pushed to increase their take. Traditional sales training and methodologies have focused on new-business selling, often to the detriment of the development of existing customers. The reality is, however, that it is usually a lot less expensive, and consequently more profitable to maintain a superior service to an existing customer, than to win a new customer. Here's why.

It Costs Less to Sell to an Existing Client

Much of the time in new-client sales is spent in courtship — convincing the potential new client that you are the sort of organisation with which they want to do business. Once they're landed, and assuming that you do an exemplary job in meeting the requirement of the first deal, the selling becomes a lot easier.

Relationship building can be formally planned and monitored in exactly the same manner as any sales or marketing campaign.

Long-Term Customers Bring Referrals

Whether these referrals are to external organisations or to other divisions of the customer organisation, they offer a valuable source of potential revenue. Referrals generally come only from longer-term customers comfortable enough to stick their necks out and recommend you.

Longer-Term Customers Will Pay More

Existing customers place a value, firstly, on the time they save in not having to re-educate suppliers on the basics of their organisation's workings each and every time they need help, and, secondly, on the lesser risk that is attached to doing business with someone they know will address their requirements in a quality fashion, on time and within the budget. This is added value, for which we'll all gladly pay.

Seven Steps to Better Customer Relationships

Relationship development is something that is generally considered to be the sole responsibility of individual sales-people. Successful relationships are often considered dependent upon the personal abilities of salespeople to establish rapport with key individuals in important accounts. It shouldn't be so. Relationship building can be formally planned and monitored in exactly the same fashion as any sales or marketing campaign — by setting firm objectives for everyone who has any contact within the key customer accounts, and by measuring performance against those objectives. A relationship-development programme should include action plans to realise the following objectives, at the very least.

1. Involve Everyone

Ensure that all customer-facing personnel:

- Know who your major customers are, and about their businesses;

- Are familiar with names of the key contacts in these customers;

- Understand those customers' priorities in terms of the products/services they source from you;

- Share the value that you place on your customers' priorities, and portray a 'partnership' approach to addressing them;

- Appreciate what makes your organisation's products/ services so special;

- View complaints as a high-priority concern and a chance to excel.

However, involving front-line personnel is only half the task. Senior management must also take responsibility for working with account-development teams to establish peer-level contact in customer accounts. That sort of contact can open doors which would otherwise remain closed to sales or support personnel, and insulates the account relationship from dependence on a single contact, such as the salesperson.

2. Know Their Business Inside Out

This level of customer knowledge is best built by those team-members who have frequent contact within the customer account — sales or support people, for example. Customers will happily provide you with the sort of information that makes this type of awareness possible. Personnel in contact with the account should continually seek input through questions like:

- What are your organisational objectives — short, medium and long term?

- What are your department's objectives?

- What part will you play in meeting these objectives?

- How might the operation of the organisation be improved?

99

- How might the operation of your department be improved?

- What do you view as the key trends in your industry?

- Whom do you consider to be your main competitors?

- How do you position yourself against these competitors?

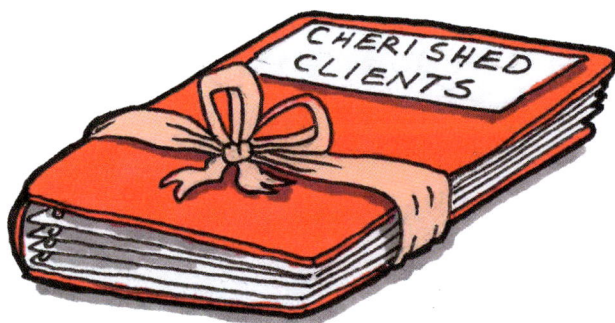

3. Know Them Personally

People make decisions that are based on who they are. Account teams should seek to understand personal ambitions and objectives — where do their contacts see themselves going in the context of their organisations; what are they trying to achieve? Can your organisation be an ally in helping them to meet their personal objectives or career aspirations? Harvey Mackay, the successful US entrepreneur and author of *Swim with the Sharks*, has a system called the 'Mackay 55' — containing at least 55 pieces of information on every one of his business's contacts. The availability of inexpensive easy-to-use online CRM systems like www.salesforce.com makes the collection and management of this sort of information much easier than it has ever been. (You can test-drive this system free of charge for 30 days. Check it out.)

4. Pulse-Check the Relationship — Frequently

Account teams must take control of relationship development, continually seeking feedback on how you and your products/services are perceived. Be sure that they're not too afraid to hear what they're doing wrong, or too modest to hear what they're doing right, asking:

- Are we living up to your expectations?

- How can we improve what we're doing for you?

- Is there anything else we should be doing to ensure our position as a favoured supplier?

- Is there anyone else within the organisation to whom you feel we should be talking?

- Who is your number-one supplier of (your kind of products/services)? Why?

- How can we become your number-one supplier?

- Who is currently providing other products/services that we could potentially supply?

- Why are these suppliers used?

- What should we do to position ourselves for this business?

- What new challenges might we be able to help you to meet?

Account teams should listen to what they're told, and be seen to act upon it — feeding back any improvements or changes made as a result of customer comments.

5. Be Their Eyes and Ears

Another way to improve relationships with key account contacts is through the unsolicited provision of information that is relevant to their personal and organisational goals — identifying materials, ideas and news that might be of practical use to them. No one has as much time as they feel they need to keep up-to-date in today's fast-moving, information-rich business world. Sources include newspapers, industry periodicals and the World Wide Web. Maintain a steady stream of value-adding communication with key account contacts. This alone can have a powerful effect in positioning you as a valued partner.

6. Thank Them — Every Time

It is not possible to overstate the impact of two such small words. Be sure that your customers are aware of the value placed on every piece of business they pass you.

7. Do it Again, and Again, and...

Make relationship maintenance and development an integral part of the way you do business. Ensure that everyone on your team understands that they must play a part in maintaining and developing good profitable relationships with your major accounts.

When almost every other aspect of your business environment is changing at a rate that makes even medium-term planning difficult, Customer Relationship Management provides a reliable link to a profitable future. Invest in it.

Strategy 16

Fast-Forward

Fast-Forward

When the Going Gets Tough...

Deals are stalled, decisions slow in coming. When you compare the current selling environment to the one we enjoyed a few, short years ago, you could be forgiven for feeling sometimes as if someone has hit the 'slow motion' button.

We have all been touched to some extent by the knock-on effect of the recent slowdown on pending sales decisions. Your products and services are still as good as they ever were, or even better — right? At least some of your customers and prospects still have a clear need for what you have on the table, and the wherewithal to do business with you. You're still doing all the right things you always did to close business and yet it's just not happening for you the way it did a few years ago.

A famous definition of insanity describes it as '*doing the same thing over and over again, but expecting a different result each time*'. Tough times change the whole sales landscape. If you're still trying to sell the same people the same propositions as you did six months ago, you could just be a little crazy. It's time to stop and take a closer look at what exactly is going with your sales opportunities.

Before continuing investment of sales time and energy for uncertain return, give your sales funnel this three-step makeover and get your sales moving at full speed again.

Step 1: Qualify Your Current Sales Forecast

Take a hard look at all of the opportunities on your current sales forecast — be ready to be very critical in qualifying their likelihood of becoming real business. Categorise every opportunity under one of these three headings:

Be very critical in qualifying the likelihood of deals in your funnel becoming real business.

1. Business that Can Be Won in the Short/Medium Term if the Right Things are Done

These are the opportunities where there is still clearly a pressing need for what you've proposed, and the will and means to do business still exists.

2. Deals that Look Doubtful Given the Recent Change in Confidence

Some of your opportunities will probably qualify as '*nice to have*', as opposed to '*must have*', in the minds of your prospect. In tighter times, these opportunities don't die — they just don't close; and the tantalising prospect of bringing them home can tempt you into investing even more time and effort in something that won't produce anything for you in the short term. Be ruthless — regardless of how much time or effort you've already invested in these deals, be prepared to face the reality that they may not close for you until things start to look a little brighter.

3. Dead Deals

Bury them. Although it can be hard to walk away, you simply can't afford a time and energy investment in hopeless cases. Stop working on them; quit investing resources in them; stop even thinking about them. Save your time, energy and resources for less hopeless cases. Take them off your forecast.

By all means, keep a watching brief on those opportunities under heading number 2, but your immediate focus must be solely upon those that were categorised under heading number 1.

Step 2: Look at the Purchase Process in Each Target Account

Now that you know which opportunities merit your fullest attention, you need to determine precisely what's going on in those accounts — what stands in the way of a decision in your favour? In good times, the power to make purchase decisions is spread far and wide within organisations, with many departments and individuals having independent spending authority. When things become as cautious as they have recently, the decision-making process changes dramatically. The level at which purchase decisions are made moves up a peg or two (or three), and a greater element of centralised structure and control ensures that every purchase directly contributes to one of two primary goals — the reduction of costs or the increasing of revenues. Suddenly, previously 'urgent' purchases are subjected to tremendous scrutiny at higher levels; and many *just-about-to-close* deals go into a sort of limbo where they neither close nor are lost — and the cash-flow effects resulting from this are what mortally wound otherwise perfectly viable sales-oriented organisations.

Before you can do anything with your best opportunities, you need to understand the game you're now in — who else is now playing, and what new rules apply?

Your first port of call must be your current 'champion(s)' or 'buyer(s)' — that person or group of people who previously had the ability to say 'Yes!' For a variety of reasons that include confusion and damaged egos, not all of your current buyers will be straight enough to inform you outright that things have changed dramatically and that they no longer hold the major sway over the decision-making process on your proposal.

There's a simple 'litmus test' that will tell you whether things have changed or not. If you suddenly find that you

can't get a direct answer regarding when your proposal will be accepted or rejected, where precisely it is in the decision-making process, or when a final decision will be made, then this unpredictability is probably coming from the fact that your buyer is no longer in control. And, if your buyer is no longer in control of the decision-making process, then your ability to affect the outcome has been seriously eroded. Think about it — if the decision is now being made a few steps further up the line, then for you to be successful, your former buyer must sell your proposition to the next level up, and so on, until it reaches the level at which a decision can be made. Continuing to sell solely to your previous buyer is more like *Chinese Whispers* than professional selling — you simply cannot be sure that your business case is going to make it up the line intact; you can't even be sure that your former positioning will even appeal to the new decision-makers.

If you find that your current account contact can't tell you where your deal is in the decision-making process, it's likely that your buyer is no longer in real control.

The only realistic way to regain some control over the process is to identify where the decision will be made and by whom — and then to set about building bridges to that/those person(s).

Your current contact will be your best source of information on who is now involved in the decision-making process. But you need to be cautious — if the decision-making authority has passed from your contact's grasp, even to a degree, they may be feeling a little raw and disempowered. The last thing they'll want to do is help you to cut them out of the process. Remember, they too have had their plans disrupted and, if what you had proposed formed part of their plans, then you share common interests — even in the new buying environment. The first thing these formerly primary contacts will need is reassurance — that you'll help them to work through the internal sales process that has resulted from the decision-making responsibility floating further up the line.

You'll need a lot of information on any changes to the decision-making process before you can decide on how to proceed from this point. At a minimum, you must find out:

- Who will now have the final say on approval of your deal?

- Who else will be involved in the decision?

- What are their particular priorities (cost-cutting, revenue improvement, strategic positioning, etc)?

- What are the new priorities for the company as a whole? (You must know precisely what is motivating your new buyers to action and precisely what is fuelling their decision-making.)

- How is your proposal currently perceived (nice to have, must have, ho-hum…)?

- What, in the eyes of these new buyers, are the perceived risks of proceeding with your proposal?

- What are their alternatives and what are the relative benefits of those?

- What do your champions think you'll need to do to keep things on track? And how can you help (preparing business cases, providing presentational support, etc)?

With this information under your belt, you now know who you should be targeting — but with what? And before you rush off into selling to any newly identified buyers, be sure that what you have to offer is going to appeal.

Step 3: Examine Your Value Proposition

When the buyer or purchase process in one of your key opportunities changes, it's key that you see how what you currently have on offer stacks up to the expectations of the new buyers.

When you first submitted your proposal, the climate within the target organisation may have been very different indeed. Previous arguments and justifications for your proposal may have become redundant — if they were not formulated to appeal to particular motivations of a new set of buyers.

With all of the understanding you have of the new decision-makers and their motivations, look critically at the business case you are currently promoting for your deal. Will it appeal to these new buyers with their different priorities?

You'll need to be convinced that your proposal stacks up under three main criteria:

Positioning

Be certain that all of your arguments and justifications will work two or three pegs higher up in the organisation — it's key that you position your offering specifically to appeal to the motivations and objectives you've identified at this loftier decision-making level.

Financial Justification

In tough economic times, there is a greater focus on the basics — like cutting costs and increasing revenues. While the issues that will have sold your original contacts may well still be important, it will now also be key that you carefully quantify the particular financial and strategic benefits that will accrue to them from implementation of your proposal. Almost all substantial purchases being made currently will be backed up by strong *Return-On-Investment* cases. An industry watcher observed: '... *most businesses are reducing the amount they are spending on products, and are only focusing on a small number of projects with a faster payback...This means that companies whose sales propositions have a strong return on investment angle are closing new sales....*' Be sure that you have a strong financial justification that addresses what you now know to be the priorities of the now higher buyers.

Differentiation

Even if your newly constituted value proposition is well positioned and financially justifiable, you could still be exposed if it suffers any element of '*me too*' — if it is not sufficiently differentiated from the propositions of other competitors who may be vying for the same business. Don't forget your basic marketing — be sure that your proposition includes strong *Unique Selling Propositions* that put you head and shoulders above any potential competitors.

Completely remodel your value proposition until you are satisfied that your 'new' proposal will fly in the new decision-making environment.

Now Get Back Out and Start Selling Again

Only now that you know what you need to sell, how best to position it, and who has to be sold, should you seek out your new buyers and begin the selling process anew.

Invest the time, energy and effort necessary to identify the potential winners in your sales pipeline; remodel your propositions to cope with changes in buying patterns; and watch your sales go *fast-forward*.

Strategy 17

Buried Treasure

Buried Treasure

Who Knows What Treasure is Hidden Right Under Your Nose?

Were you ever going through the pockets of a jacket you knew you had but hadn't worn in a while (*or through an off-shore account you had forgotten about?!*) when you found a few Euros you didn't realise you had? It feels pretty good, finding something of value where you least expected it, doesn't it?

Well, that experience is there to be had when you take a fresh look through the team of people that makes up your staff — extra value that you had forgotten was there (or never knew about in the first place) which, when you identify it, gives you a whole new view of your business. We all today subscribe to the idea that 'our people are our greatest asset', recognising that those organisations who stand head and shoulders above our peers and competitors in business tend to have superior people policies and, on the face of it, superior people. Accordingly, many of us spend a huge amount of time chasing the rainbow, at the end of which we know we'll find a pot full of those perfect people that our industry leaders seem to have, instead of focusing upon identifying the best in those who already make up our teams. And therein lies the secret of those organisations that have people-based competitive advantage — it's not just that they identify and recruit great people (and, of course, that does help), but that they work with those people that they have to make them great — to find just what attributes they uniquely possess that can be developed and

> *Successful organisations work with their existing people to make them world-class.*

employed effectively within the organisation, to build the sort of serious competitive advantage that only good people can confer.

8, 11, 15, 5, 14, 1, 7, 6, 10, 13, 3, 12, 2 — what's the pattern in this series of numbers? Take a moment to look it over, and then, if you're stumped, turn quickly to the box at the end of this strategy for the answer. Then, read on.

So what? Well, the simple point is that sometimes looking at the familiar in an entirely different way can produce results that we scarcely expect. Your people are like that — you assume that because you've worked with them for a while, you know what they are, and what they're capable of. That's only true up to a point. To uncover genuine hidden potential requires a phase shift in the way you look at your people.

Take the following actions to get you started.

Uncover Your Team's Career Goals, Aspirations Likes/Dislikes and Strengths/Weaknesses

You can't begin this process without knowing a lot about each and every member of your team. Start by talking with them regularly. Find out what it is they *like* to do. Research published in *Harvard Business Review* ('Job Sculpting', *HBR*,

Sept–Oct 1999) demonstrated that people excel at jobs that interest them deeply more than at jobs that their education, skills or experience might suggest are perfect fits for them. Find out what your people enjoy doing, what career plans each has, and where they aspire to go in your business or in life in general. Don't confine yourself to informal chats. Use more formal means like the Profiles *Checkpoint Multi-rater* system (www.profilesinternational.com) and psychometric assessments like the *Profile XT* to determine the particular strengths of your key assets. The authors of the *HBR* research cited above put it perfectly: '...*the best way to keep your stars is to know them better than they know themselves — and then use that information to customize the career of their dreams.*'

Make Better Use of Strengths

When you have a good appreciation of the particular strengths of each member of your team, start to look for new ways in which to apply them. Brainstorm on how you can apply these strengths in new or imaginative ways to enhance the roles of each of your people and to address problems that you haven't previously been able to address. Don't be hemmed in by '*This is the way we usually do things*' or by rigid job descriptions or functional demarcations. In one successful example we observed recently in the IT industry, a talented project manager was put into the role of sales manager — not because she knew an awful lot about sales or had a gleaming sales record — quite the contrary — but because she was particularly good at organising campaigns, marshalling resources, motivating her team to action, and seeing initiatives through to the end. Take off the blinkers when it comes to applying strengths in new ways.

Turn Weaknesses into Strengths

In the movie, *Enemy of the State*, Gene Hackman tells Will Smith — '*...in guerrilla warfare you gotta turn your strengths into weaknesses...if they're big and you're small, then you're fast and they're slow...you've got to work with what you've got*'. You've got to do the same with your people. Look at what you currently perceive or complain about as shortcomings, and then look at situations where those attributes could be positive — after all, most weaknesses are just overused strengths. For example, a Customer Service Representative who's just too assertive to 'put up and shut up' with angry clients may actually make a very successful salesperson, capable of overcoming objections not easily overcome by others. Or consider the marketing executive who comes up with killer campaigns but just can't seem to follow them through to the end — focus that person solely on developing the creative campaigns, and assign project management and completion to someone better suited. Look at every shortcoming you currently perceive in your team-members, figure out where that weakness might become a strength, and figure out how you can capitalise upon it. You'll be amazed at the results.

Feedback, Feedback, Feedback

In a recent Profiles International study of the reasons why people leave their jobs, Profiles found that, of the several hundred people surveyed, more than 25 per cent cited one of the main reasons for changing jobs as lack of feedback from management on their performance. Make it a formal objective to provide positive feedback on a job well done to every one of your people at least weekly. This means a mind-set where you and your management team are actively seeking opportunities to provide feedback. Not only does this increase the interest level in the job being done (we all like to be recognised), but it really helps to reinforce positive behaviours and performance at the expense of more negative alternatives. Also, experience shows that when you feed back to your team, they'll feed back to you — on all of the ways in which you can work with them more effectively.

If you've been searching for an unassailable competitive advantage, then the answer may be just under your nose — before you start exploring more exotic sources, look at the people who are driving your company right now. You'll find that there's untold treasure buried behind those familiar faces you meet every day.

Pattern in the Numbers?

Being familiar with numbers and number-series puzzles, the natural inclination is to calculate the mathematical relationship between 8 and 11, and then between 11 and 15, and so on until you can speculate as to the mathematical progression — and there is none! The numbers are arranged alphabetically! Look just a little differently at your people, who are so familiar to you, and learn an awful lot more about what can make them great for you and your organisation.

* Thanks to Donna Engelson for this teaser.

Strategy 18

Death Valley

Death Valley

Cut Your Sales Cycle by Half

Would you like to save time, shorten your sales cycle, and close a larger percentage of the first-time appointments you make? You are about to learn a sales technique that takes no time or effort to implement — but one that will dramatically improve your hit rate.

First, let us take you back to a sales meeting in your past …you meet a prospective client for the first time on a Tuesday, and absolutely everything goes great. You effectively engage the prospect; everything 'clicks' personally; your discovery process uncovers her needs clearly; and you discuss an outline solution that she's enthusiastic about. All in all, the call could not have gone better. You agree with your enthused future client that you'll summarise the discussion in a proposal within days — with a view to calling the following week to follow up. Sounds spot on, doesn't it?

The clock is now ticking. You don't have a wildly busy week so you get the proposal started on Wednesday, and finished and in the post on Thursday. No point phoning on Friday — even if the postal service did a first-class job, you know that she won't have had a chance to absorb it yet. Best to wait until the following week. You actually estimate your proposal will arrive on Monday, so you put in the first call on Tuesday. You leave your first voice mail and, so that you 'don't seem too hungry or pushy', you leave it until Wednesday, or even Thursday, to follow up again. On Thursday or Friday, you breach the dreaded voice-mail defences and get to speak to your prospect for the first time since your initial meeting, which is already nine or ten days in the past.

Your prospect has had a *'chance to glance through it but not really give it the attention it deserves'* (you know she hasn't even looked at it yet but that's OK) and requests that you call early next week to follow up again. 'Monday would look too desperate' so you leave it until Tuesday to phone again. If you're lucky, you get through first time; if not,

> *Death Valley: that dry dead-man's zone that stretches from first contact to proposal follow-up*

you try again with the voice mails and follow-ups. Eventually, earliest Tuesday, or more likely later that week, you get to talk to the prospect about your proposal. It's now more than two weeks since you first met. She seems vague, cool, and anything but as enthusiastic as she was when she suggested you prepare the proposal at that sales meeting that sent you dancing between the raindrops back to your office. She suggests that you *'leave it with her'* and she'll *'get back to you'*. Time passes and she slips from your prospect list — never to be heard from again.

121

What happened? You fell into the biggest trap in sales. You wandered unwittingly into Death Valley — that dry zone that stretches from first contact to proposal follow-up. All around are the bleaching bones of the countless millions of salespeople who preceded you.

Another thin-on-the-ground opportunity bites the dust.

The conventional wisdom in selling suggests that this is an unavoidable consequence of selling — one of the elements in the 'numbers game' that you just have to learn to swallow. Not true!

Make one simple change to your sales call right now and you can fix this problem forever. **Every single time you meet a prospect, make the next appointment before you leave.** That's it — simple but highly effective. Suppose it's your first appointment and you've agreed to prepare a proposal — don't leave without looking for an appointment to meet with the prospect again to bring the proposal back in to talk it through, within days if possible.

There are a few possible responses when you try to set the next appointment for a few days later.

1. She Agrees

You are already winning. For a start, you've qualified her interest ('Always Be Closing'). If she's prepared to meet you again, her interest looks genuine and you've immediately hacked a few weeks off your sales cycle. Also, your positive initial meeting won't have time to slip her mind. When you next meet, she remembers why she was so enthusiastic about what you had to say, how you planned to meet her pressing requirements, and why she asked you to prepare a proposal for her. What sales-person wouldn't close more of those deals than the Death Valley specials above?

2. She Declines

'*You know, the rest of my week is just completely full.*' You suggest early the following week, but '*next week is even worse*'. You push for the week after that again, and she suggests that you '*simply post in your proposal*'. It seems that she

> Every single time you meet a prospect, make the next appointment before you leave.

doesn't want to solve the problem you've discussed badly enough to want to see you again. So, maybe you haven't done a good enough job of uncovering her real require-ments and creating a vision of the way in which you can help her meet them; or she's not the real buying decision-maker; or she doesn't have the budget.

Even this is good news — because now you have infor-mation you didn't previously have. If you feel you've got the right person, right requirements, and an existing budget, then you can flip back into the discovery process and try to recover things.

If you've got the wrong person, then you can probe for the right one and start over with her instead.

If it's simply a hopeless case, then, when you get outside, slap yourself on the back — you just saved yourself the time, energy and effort of preparing a proposal; the time and cost of numerous phone calls; and the disappointment as another one bites the dust. You've just saved time that you can use with more worthy prospects.

You win something every time you ask for the next appointment on the current appointment — more information, more clarity, more time, or an earlier chance to opt out of a doomed sales opportunity.

Make this simple change to your sales process right away and soar over your competitors' bones in Death Valley.

Strategy 19

Cold Comfort

Cold Comfort

Warm Up Your Cold Calls

Ever had a 100lb phone? Anyone who ever has to sell knows how it feels for their phone to be so heavy that they can't pick it up to cold-call a list of potential prospects.

This 'cold-call reluctance' generally stems from one of two main sources — fear of rejection or lack of preparation.

You'll Never be Rejected on a Cold Call

We all have fragile egos — to a greater or lesser extent. Nobody likes to be rejected. Anyone making cold calls needs to realise that the person at the far end of the phone has no idea who you are, whether you're a tough or a wimp, or whether you're a nice person — they simply don't have enough information to reject you. So, when they cut the call short or don't respond to your pitch, they are rejecting what you're offering — and that's got nothing to do with you personally. Give yourself a break — shake it off. Remember that you are playing a numbers game, and every 'no' gets you closer to your next 'yes'. Anyway, if you were adequately prepared before making the call, then you know that that person could have benefitted greatly from doing business with you — it's their loss. So there's nothing to beat yourself up about — unless you were unprepared.

126

The following tips will ensure that you'll be so well prepared that cold-call reluctance will become a thing of the past.

What's in it for Me?

Everyone thinks, '*What's in it for me?*' Crystallise the particular benefits that your product or service will bring to your prospects, and be so convinced by these benefits that you are anxious to share this information with anyone you can.

How will this prospect benefit from what we offer? How soon will these benefits come? What will it mean to them — will their businesses run better, sell more, provide better customer survive, reduce costs, or increase productivity? Why should they be excited by what I have to tell them? Once you know this, you'll find that you begin to want to make those calls — but don't rush off yet...

> *Anyone making cold calls must realise that the person at the end of the phone doesn't have enough information to reject them personally.*

Know Precisely What You Want to Achieve Before You Make Any Call

Precisely what action do you want your target to take? Decide upon your primary objective for the call, and then set fall-back objectives. For example, your primary objective when you call might be to get an appointment in the diary to meet with them. Your first fall-back might be an agreement that you'll call again the following week to put the

127

appointment in the diary, and a further fall-back that you'll call them to talk again once they have a chance to read some collateral you'll send them on by post. Be clear in what you want to achieve with every call you make — and have decided at what point you'll abandon one objective for the next desirable outcome.

Grab Their Interest Quickly

If you received a call from yourself, what would drive everything else from your mind long enough for you to tune in to the rest of the call? Come up with a statement or question that slaps your prospects in the face and makes them concentrate on what you have to say. For example, a colleague who works with a mobile-phone operator boldly tells every Financial Director they speak with, '*We can cut your mobile-phone bills by more than 30 per cent TODAY.*' Snatch their attention.

Ask Questions that Force Them to Think

Think of all of the main benefits your prospects would get from doing business with you and ask questions related to these benefits that get them thinking. For example, '*How much would a 30 per cent reduction in your mobile-phone bills save you on a monthly basis?*' Engage them.

Get to the Point

Engage in conversation for only as long as it takes to hook your prospect's interest. Then ask for what you've called to get — be it an appointment, a sale, or whatever. Don't be drawn into longer conversations with those who hit it off with you on the phone — the longer the call, the more opportunity for rejection. Take only as long as it takes to get to the point where you feel your prospect is ready to move to the next step with you. Then bring the call to a close. Go for the gold early.

Get the First Call Over Quickly

Prospecting calls are like a boulder sitting atop a hill — until you give it a push, it could stay there for millennia. But put your back behind it, push it over the edge, and soon it's hurtling down the hill at breakneck speed. The first call each day is the push that gets you going. If you have any way of grading your calls according to their likely success, start with the least important first — do your warm-up with your lesser prospects. Once the first is out of the way, things get a little easier — go straight into the second and work your way to the end of your call list. Get a rhythm and go with it.

Don't get drawn into long conversations — the longer the call, the more opportunity for rejection.

Lighten your phone — be sure to prepare carefully any time you have to make cold calls, and give yourself a break when you get a 'No!' Take comfort from the fact that there will always be some people too misguided to see how much you could have done for them.

129

'If you're not
getting enough
"No" answers,
you're not getting
out there enough.'

STEPHEN SCHIFFMAN
COLD CALLING TECHNIQUES

Strategy 20

Examine Your Conscience

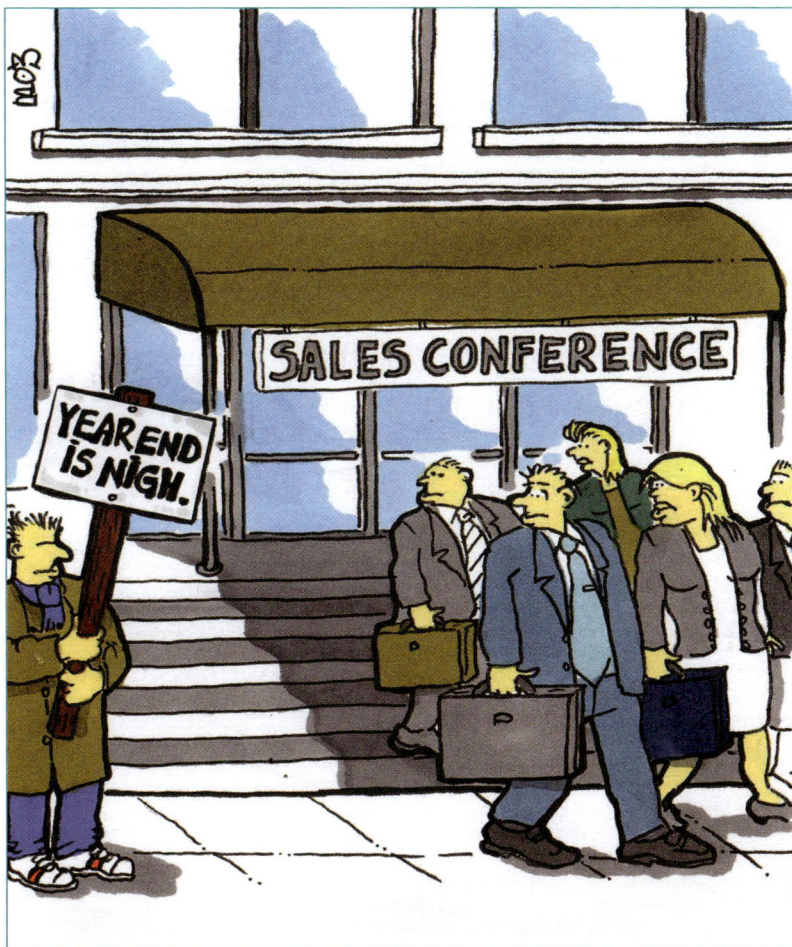

Examine Your Conscience

Repent! Ye Sales Sinners!

For businesspeople, sales is the pre-Galilean planet around which all of the universe revolves. No sales, no business. When sales start to go off track, it is usually because we've committed one or other of the sales sins below. Do a quick decade of sales meditations and clear your conscience. Are you or your salespeople guilty of any of the following?

I. Forgetting that Sales is a Numbers Game

Research shows that most successful salespeople spend as little as one-third of their time actually selling. The other two-thirds is spent in cultivating leads and prospects that will ensure that they have plenty of good selling opportunities available to them on an ongoing basis. Salespeople fail when the pipeline dries up.

Examine your conscience: Are you working consistently hard to keep a constant flow of leads and prospects in the pipeline or are you relying upon pot luck?

II. Giving Up Too Early

A major study showed that:

- 48 per cent of salespeople make one call and stop;

- 25 per cent of salespeople make two calls and stop;

- 15 per cent of salespeople make three calls and stop;

- 12 per cent of all salespeople go back and back and back and back.

Not surprisingly, the study also found that it is this latter 12 per cent who make most of the sales!

Search your heart: Do you ever give up too quickly?

III. Making Friends, Not Prospects

The originators of *relationship* marketing and selling have a lot

Successful salespeople spend two-thirds of their time cultivating leads and prospects— do you?

to answer for — it's just so easy to justify the time you spend with people you like or people who like you. Don't fool yourself — the people you like are not always the best prospects and, while looking to development of good relationships with all of your contacts is laudable, much more important is clear focus upon what each and every one of them will deliver to your bottom line.

Be honest: Is it the value of prospective business or the warmth and comfort of a relationship that drives your interest in prospects?

IV. Talking More than the Prospect

The more your prospect talks, the more you learn. The more you learn, the better your chance of winning the business. The most successful salespeople facilitate a process whereby the customer becomes so involved in the sales process that they do most of the talking — the salesperson simply becomes a facilitator.

> Spend your time with the best prospects — not the prospects you like best.

Tell the truth: When you look at your sales calls, who's doing 95 per cent of the talking?

V. Not Learning the Prospect's Business

You can tell when the salesperson trying desperately to part you from your money has learned enough about your business to make a useful contribution to its development. Your prospects are no different. Fail to learn the prospect's business and, regardless of the super relationship you've built, the register rings 'No Sale!'

Ponder:
Am I taking the time to learn my prospects' businesses?

VI. Not Winning the Customer's Confidence

Prospects don't completely believe in your PR, advertising, or product copy — they believe in people. You are your product. Fail to win their confidence and you'll fail to sell. It's that simple.

Look into your soul: Do I communicate an honest, professional, capable partner that my prospects can rely upon?

VII. Not Selling the Company

Even the most seasoned salesperson can sometimes forget that even when they have successfully sold their own bona fides and those of their products, the prospect is still going to be concerned about what's behind the scenes supporting them. They'll think: *'What happens to me if this guy is gone tomorrow?'* There are always three sales to be made — the products, the salesperson and the credibility and reliability of the company behind them.

Tell the truth: Do you always focus on making all three sales — me, my products AND my company?

VIII. Not Joining the Customer's Team

It's no longer enough to have good-quality products and services — everyone has that. Prospects today want knowledgeable, effective and consultative partners who will contribute some additional knowledge and expertise to their team. Helping customers directly to address business challenges is what makes the difference between pedlar and consultant.

Meditate: If I were gone tomorrow, would my customers miss my expertise in their business?

IX. Not Creating a 'Benefits Vision' for the Customer

In order to buy, we all need to have a clear picture of the many benefits that will accrue to us from anything we purchase. The most successful salespeople work hard to build in the minds of their customers a clear, compelling vision of the benefits of everything they sell. This clear mental picture of a 'happiest ever after' scenario is key to consistent sales success.

Search your heart: Do my presentations evoke an emotional response — can my prospect clearly visualise the benefits of buying from me?

X. Not Going that Extra Mile

Everyone is at their best when they are on the brink of closing a deal with a prospect — especially the first deal. We'll all do our level best to ensure that we satisfy every one of our prospect's demands at this key stage. That's why no one is overly impressed by extra effort at sales time — it's the norm for you and for all of your competitors. What counts is how you behave when the sale is done. Do you deliver? Do you keep your promises? Do you live up to expectations by keeping promises and ensuring that your customer gets a return on whatever they buy from you? Are you still around delivering real business value between sales? If your follow through is poor, so will your follow-up sales be poor.

Examine your conscience: Am I known for consistent world-class follow through?

Keep your conscience clear and your selling religiously free of these sales sins, and see your business soar to heavenly heights.

Strategy 21

A Perfect Pitch...

A Perfect Pitch...

Creating the Perfect Pitch

Research shows that most people fear making a public presentation more than they fear death — the majority of funeral attendees would rather be in the casket than up delivering the eulogy!

That's because most of us have bought into the myth that '*Good presenters are born, not made.*' Sure, there are some people who have certain natural abilities that make presentations easier for them — but, with the necessary application, anyone can become a great presenter. To paraphrase Thomas Edison: '*Great presentations are 10% inspiration and 90% perspiration*' — and the perspiration in presentation is preparation, preparation, preparation.

Next time you have a key presentation coming up, be sure to include these key steps in your preparation.

1. Don't Talk to Strangers

You haven't a hope of persuading an audience you don't know. You must know all that you can about your target audience — *What are their backgrounds? What are their concerns? What will turn them on? What will turn them off?*

Where do they stand on the topic you're presenting? How much do they know about your topic? Know your audience inside out.

2. Begin with the End in Mind

Before you even think about preparing your killer presentation, you've got to clarify precisely what it is that you intend this presentation to achieve. You've got to ask yourself, 'What do I want my audience to do when I've fin-

> *Great presentations are 10% inspiration and 90% perspiration.*

ished making my pitch — and what will make them want to do that?' Expand that further to determine: *What's your key message? What's in it for the audience (what are the benefits of what I'm proposing to the audience?) What might prevent them from taking my advice? What precise action do I want them to take as a result of my presentation, and when?*

3. Structure Your Presentation

Before you run off to start up Powerpoint, be sure that you have a compelling structure on the ideas you plan to outline in your presentation. A *Problem–Analysis–Solution* approach will work for every presentation, and ensures that your presentation has a structure that even the slowest member of your audience will be able to follow.

● First, Identify a Problem

The problem is the issue that has you on your feet presenting. Identify the problem that your audience needs solved. Maybe it's a problem they already recognise; but, more likely, you are setting out to provide them with a solution to a problem they haven't yet recognised — perhaps they need a new product or service to improve something they already do, or perhaps you need them to adopt a new marketing strategy to maximise their return on marketing investment. Whatever issue your presentation is addressing must be understood clearly by every member of your audience right from the start. First, define the problem.

- ● Second, Analyse the Problem

  Now, use facts, figures, and clear examples to explain the background to the problem, why it exists, what impact it's having on the day-to-day lives of your audience, and why it needs to be addressed.

- ● Then, Provide a Solution

  If you've done a good job with the first two steps, your audience is waiting for you to provide a solution to the problem you've outlined and analysed. Be sure that your solution is carefully formulated to address all of the issues raised in the previous two steps.

Base all of your presentations on this simple three-step process and your audience will instinctively understand where you're going with your presentation — and will go there with you more easily.

4. Build Your Presentation

With the advent of effective and affordable software packages like Powerpoint, it has never been easier to build an attractive presentation. Be sure, however, that your Powerpoint software supports your presentation — and does not dominate it. Here are some general guidelines for the effective use of presentation software and other aids:

- Keep your slide content in brief bullets, and try to keep to about four bullets per slide;

- Avoid the clip art that comes with your package — most people will have seen it already and will find it boringly familiar. If you must use clip art, source some more interesting stuff on one of the many websites dedicated to the subject (Microsoft's own online clip-art site is outstanding);

- Be wary of animated titles or clip art — they can distract from the message;

- Leave out bullet-point sound effects like sirens, skidding tires, typewriting, laughing or applauding. They are distracting and amateur;

- Use video clips only if they are good quality and add something to your presentation that you can add in no other way — again, they can tend to distract;

- Choose simple fonts and basic primary-colour schemes;

- Give your slides headlines, not titles — use them to summarise the key message in each slide. For example, 'Better staff recognition means greater retention' *v.* 'Staff Recognition Strategy';

- When you've finished with a slide, don't leave it on display — particularly if the presentation/discussion has

moved on. Your audience will still sit there analysing that slide instead of listening to you;

- Leave the gadgets in your desk — there's nothing a laser pointer can do that your hand can't do more effectively. And it's distracting — you'll get more enquiries about where you bought your pointer than about your presentation. Dump the laser.

5. Polish Your Presentation

Think you're finished? Not nearly! All you've got now is the first draft — and that's what it will remain until you polish it. Before you set about polishing your presentation, revert back to the objectives you set for your presentation in Step 2 — and think about the problem you set out to solve following the advice in Step 3 above. Now, with a clear view of your objectives for the presentation, review your first draft as follows:

1. The 'So What?' Test

Look at every slide bullet and every point you make. If any of them don't contribute positively to the objective of the presentation — if you suspect that your audience might think 'So what?' — then cut it. Unnecessary points find their way into every presentation and only increase the burden on the audience. Be ruthless in your editing.

2. Does it Flow?

You've established a problem, analysed it, and then suggested how you can solve it. Does your presentation run in a straight line through these three key milestones? If it goes off track at all, cut the detours. You've told your

142

audience the problem you're going to solve — stick to the point and make it easy for them to follow you straight to your logical solution.

Leave out fancy animations, sound effects, fancy fonts and wild colours — don't lose your message in your medium.

3. Are You Repeating Yourself?

Another common error is saying the same thing too many times. Sure, repetition can drive a point home; just be sure that your presentation is not weighed down by confusing redundancies.

4. Supporting Facts

Have you enough hard facts and figures to back up your key points? Opinions are valuable, but examples, facts and figures will drive your key points home more effectively.

Congratulations! You've just completed a tightly argued and compelling presentation. Next, we'll look at how you practise it to perfection, create a high-impact opening statement to make a great first impression, pace yourself, interact with your audience effectively, and handle difficult audience members.

'Tell them what you're going to tell them; then tell them; then tell them what you told them.'

ANON

Strategy 22

...Pitched Perfectly

Pitched Perfectly...

Perfecting Your Pitching

In the last strategy, we looked at the careful preparation and polishing of a closely argued and effective presentation. Now it's time to practise it to perfection, create a high-impact opening statement to make a great first impression, pace yourself, learn how to interact with your audience effectively, and look at handling difficult audience members

Practise, Practise, Practise

Once you've got your presentation finished, the key to success is plenty of practice. This means running through the presentation, as if in front of an audience, until you have it down to a fine art. At that point, it's time to bring in a coach. If it's a truly key presentation, get a professional coach involved — the small investment in a professional's time will pay off big dividends in the end product. If you don't have the time or money for a professional coach, run your presentation past several trusted colleagues who understand the audience and your objectives. Look for lots of feedback on how you could improve the impact of the presentation. Don't ever proceed with a presentation without running it past someone's critical eye — even if they don't know your business too well, they'll spot gaps and flaws that you would otherwise miss.

The First Four Minutes

A few years back, there was a book around called *The First Four Minutes*, which explained how salespeople have just four minutes to make or lose that key sale — their prospects unconsciously decide whether or not they'll con-

> *You don't get a second chance to make a first impression — you've got four minutes!*

sider buying from them in the first four minutes of the conversation. Fail to grab the prospect's attention positively in the first four minutes and it's all over. It's not like that with presentations. You don't have that long — it's more like ten to thirty seconds! All other things being equal, your opening comments are really what determine the success or otherwise of your presentation. Your first statements must be strong and clear and must grab your audience's attention immediately — otherwise the rest of your presentation is lost.

Think of the key message that you want your presentation to convey and condense it into a brief, powerful opening. Make your opening statement truly startling — get them thinking. One of the most effective ways to open a presentation is to go straight into a true (or, at least, credible) story or parable that makes your key point for you. People like stories. Be warned, however, unless you are 100 per cent confident that you can predict your audience's reaction, and unless you are sure that you handle a really pacy delivery, forget the age-old advice to begin with a joke

147

or funny story. As presentation openings, they fail more often than they succeed — leaving a truly lasting impression when they go down in flames. Be sure to invest as much time and effort as is necessary to come up with an opening that grabs the audience immediately.

Finally, never start into your killer opening until you're sure that you have everyone's attention and complete silence. Remember that every audience can be settled with a patient and relaxed '*sssshhhhh*'. It works every time. Use it.

Move Quickly, Speak Slowly

People become bored with presentations when the pace of idea presentation is such that their minds have time to wander between ideas. Be sure to keep the development and presentation of your ideas and arguments moving along at a decent pace — get to your points quickly. However, while you want to keep the flow of ideas flowing snappily, be careful not to speak too quickly. If you speak too quickly, or run your words into one another, you'll lose the audience. When you practise and deliver your presentation, remember that what sounds to you like extremely slow delivery rarely is — it's almost impossible to speak too slowly in a pitch situation. If in doubt, slow your speech down, pausing briefly after every word. Use variations of pace, volume and tone, or even short silences to emphasise key points.

Interact With Your Audience

This is a real double-edged sword — dangerous but highly effective. Dangerous? The problem with getting your audience involved in your presentation is that, unless you're pretty experienced at presentation and audience management, they can take over and run your presentation off the rails with discussions and conversations having no relevance to the topic at hand. Effective? Involve your audience and the presentation becomes theirs — if they help make your points, then they can more easily buy into them. Combine Dale Carnegie's advice to '*Get them saying "Yes, Yes" immediately*', with the lawyers' rule — '*Never ask a question you don't know the answer to*' — and you get an effective way of involving your audience in your presentation, without allowing them control over its direction. Simply confine your audience interactions to exercises like shows of hands and responses to questions you know they'll agree/disagree with. That way, your audience will pave the way to points you have planned to introduce later in the presentation.

Be Sure to Expect Disagreement

No matter how good your presentation is or how well structured your arguments are, someone will not agree with some elements of what you say. Expect to hear from these folks when, flushed with success at reaching a successful conclusion to your presentation, you invite questions.

When you are preparing, reviewing or rehearsing your presentation, take a note of any point likely to generate disagreement. Be sure to include every controversial point.

When you have a comprehensive list of likely flash points, develop positive responses to them. Prepare and practise these until they flow as easily as the rest of the presentation.

When it comes to responding to a disagreement from an audience member, there are a few basic rules. First, pause, and be seen to think and consider what is — to the questioner,

149

at least — an important issue. After a few moments, restate the questioner's issue, ensuring that you include all of the emotional content that they've put into their point — show that you understand and appreciate their point of view even if you don't necessarily agree with it. Then, disagree in an agreeable fashion. Deliver your prepared alternative view. Don't be argumentative or heated in your response — which should be addressed to the whole audience, not to the original questioner. Make a particular point of finishing by making eye contact with someone other than the questioner. Finally, don't ask, 'Did I answer your question?' — you're only encouraging an ongoing two-way conversation at the expense of the rest of the audience. Address the issue and move on.

The Best Way to Win an Argument...

Finally, never ever get into an argument. Although you may not always be aware of it, in the eyes of your audience, you are an 'expert'. To them, you'll often have a psychological advantage over someone who disagrees with you, and, if an argument develops, you begin slightly ahead. Unfortunately for you, most people will tend to take the side of the under-dog in any argument — and this is rarely the well-prepared presenter. As ever, the best way to win an argument is to avoid it. Arguments with audience members are a lose–lose proposition — even if you win the battle, you lose the war.

So much of today's business depends upon a good pitch that it's amazing just how many presenters choose not to invest that little extra effort in turning a *ho-hum* into a *wow*!

Follow this straightforward approach and hit perfect pitch — every time.

Strategy 23

Just Say 'No!'

Just Say, 'No!'

Choose Your Battles Carefully

There never seem to be enough good deals around, with the result that when an opportunity raises its head, you automatically find yourself off and running, working hard to win the business — each and every time. It's a knee-jerk reaction. But what if the target business isn't suited to the profile of your company? What if you can't possibly win the business? Or what if winning that business is going to have some negative 'knock-on' effect on an existing valued client or project? What then?

Unless it becomes your standard practice to make a formal bid/no-bid decision on every opportunity you uncover, you will never have any reasonable way of controlling, and improving, the level of return you achieve on the investment you make in preparing and selling your business proposals. You must make a 'bid/no-bid' decision every time, and not be afraid to 'Just say, "No"' when circumstance demands it.

Why Bother with a 'Bid/No-Bid' Decision?

Every deal you chase, win or lose, costs you in a lot of obvious ways, but it also costs you in other ways which you may not previously have considered.

Financial Costs

These are obvious — all of the costs associated with proposal preparation (man-hours cost, consumables costs, etc.) are marketing costs, and are just as real as those associated with advertising, PR, brochure production, mailing and so on. Think of the time you spend before you commit to spending on any of these more obvious marketing expenses — shouldn't you think carefully before jumping in and chasing every opportunity that comes your way?

> *Run a bid/no-bid analysis on every major opportunity that comes your way — it will save you time, money and heartache.*

Less Obvious Costs

What about the less obvious, less tangible costs of chasing unsuitable business?

- **Opportunity Cost**

  What other, more profitable business might you have won and delivered if you weren't wasting your time on patently unsuitable deal opportunities?

- **Confidence Cost**

  How does the team feel if it loses deal after deal, even if it's because the opportunity wasn't really suitable? Unnecessary lost deals hurt team morale and drive. Avoid them.

- **Profile Cost**

  How does it look to the market when you are seen to chase multiple opportunities and win only a small percentage? How does it look if you pursue every

153

opportunity that comes your way — what positioning message does it send about the business you're in?

How Do You Make the 'Bid/No-Bid' Decision?

Analyse every opportunity using the following straightforward three-step procedure:

1. Use a 'Bid/No-Bid Questionnaire' to Qualify

Produce a standard 'Bid/No-Bid Questionnaire' to help you in qualifying opportunities. Be satisfied that every opportunity tests well on every count before even considering investing in pursuing business. Your questionnaire should include at least the following questions:

- Where has the opportunity come from?

- Are we technically capable of doing the work?

- Will we need extra resources (people or equipment, etc.) to complete this work and can we cost to cover this?

- Is this our kind of work? Does it send the right message to existing and prospective clients?

- Do we particularly want this work/client? Will it help to put our company 'on the map'?

- Who is our competition on this deal? Can we beat them?

- If we do win, how will this affect current business commitments?

- In landing this deal, might we lose or upset an existing, valued client or some other prospective business?

- Could we achieve a better return on our investment of time, effort and cost in preparing this proposal if we focused our energies on other opportunities?

- Is the opportunity 'rigged' for some other supplier? Are we just 'making up the numbers'?

- Is this a 'decoy' opportunity (see Strategy 28) — an opportunity formulated by the client to get some free research/consultation, or to help build a specification for a project to be undertaken in-house?

- Is there is a definite budget for this project?

- What is the prospect's payment/credit record? Can we afford to do business with them?

2. Confirm that Your Proposed Solution Has a 'Unique Selling Proposition' (USP)

For those unfamiliar with the concept, a 'Unique Selling Proposition' (USP) is some aspect of what you are offering which is absolutely unique to your proposal. If you don't have at least one strong USP, save your efforts for those proposals where you do.

3. Before Making a 'No-Bid' Decision, Ensure that there are No Extraordinary Reasons to Proceed

There will be deals that you will decide to pursue even though the testing described above suggests that they are unsuitable or un-winnable. You might decide to go after them for a variety of good reasons. For example:

- To 'Stay on the List'

  Be careful, though — a poorly prepared proposal which obviously was not submitted to win, or which does not display your customary attention to detail, may be worse than no proposal at all.

- ● Learning Curve

  You may feel that the opportunity to learn just how this client's business ticks and how best to approach such a client may be of use to you in pursuing other players in the same sector.

- ● Positioning/Profiling

  Perhaps your strategic marketing positioning is such that you cannot be seen not to bid; or maybe you simply want to raise your profile in the target client organisation.

The Bottom Line

In the end, the bid/no-bid decision-making process can be distilled to four basic questions that you should use to test all opportunities:

- ● Is this opportunity real?

- ● Can we win the business?

- ● If we do win, will it be worthwhile?

- ● If we can't win the business, is there some other very good reason to bid?

Consider these questions every time you consider an opportunity and you are taking conscious control of your proposal hit rate. But when the process tells you that an opportunity is simply not right for you, just say, 'No' ('… but thank you').

Strategy 24

Look into the Future

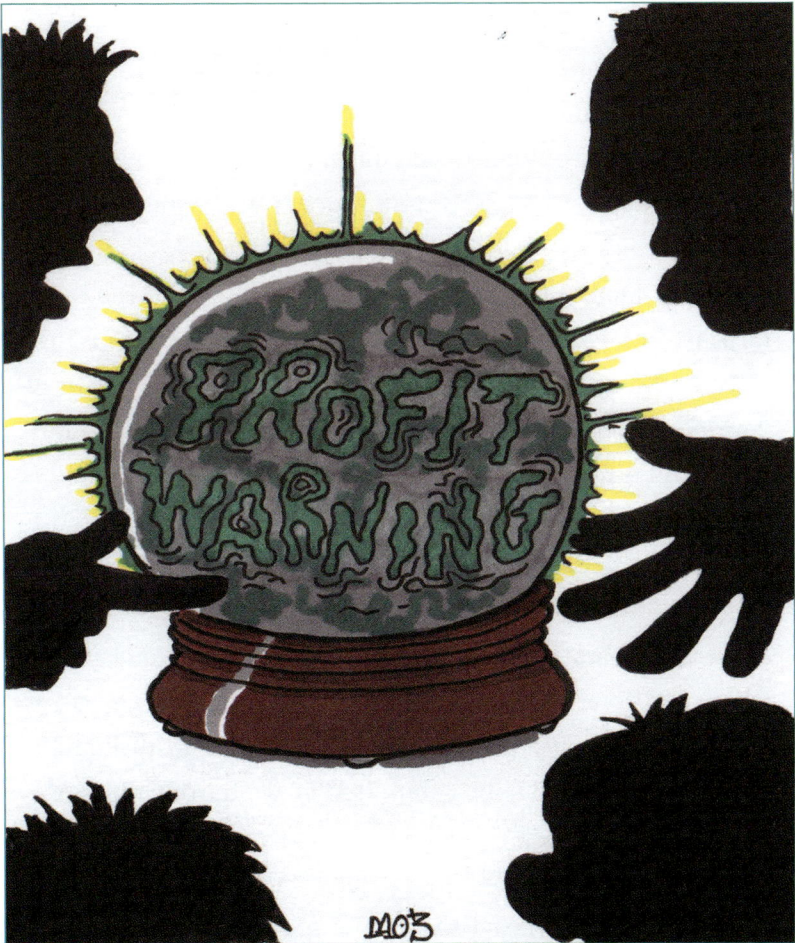

Look into the Future

Are You on Track?

First and second quarter is a great time of year! Far enough into your killer business plan to see really bright prospects for the year — yet far enough from end of year to be still utterly convinced that absolutely everything you've planned will work — and produce the great year you deserve.

At the heart of this optimistic enthusiasm is the sales forecast that is the backbone of your business plan — representing the only truly important measure of the worth of your plan — the projection of what you'll sell, in what quantities, and at what margin, to whom.

Examine your conscience — have you ever prepared a forecast that ultimately didn't pan out? Anyone who tells you they haven't is either delusional or is riding a wave of so-far lucky statistics towards a fall. Even in good years, where sufficient revenues are achieved, the majority of sales forecasts are poor predictors of what is ultimately sold, when and to whom — but, hell, if we hit our numbers, it no longer matters, right? Maybe in former years it didn't, but not in the new economy. No longer can any of us afford the luxury of a forecast that is not absolutely airtight — a truly reliable predictor of the outcome of all of the time, money and effort we plan investing in our businesses. So don't take chances. Review your sales forecast for reality — while there's still time to do something about any chinks that you find in your armour.

Let's assume that your forecast consists of sales into existing and new accounts — sales you hope you'll make from beating the bushes for suspects, and sales that are already in process to some extent or other. In this strategy, we'll look at new business sales; in Strategy 25, we'll come back to reality checking sales that have already made it from your suspect to your prospect list.

At the core of a successful sales plan is a sales forecast that provides an optimistic backbone to support your efforts.

So, let's get going on a four-question reality check of your new business forecast.

Question 1: What are Your Projected Sales?

Look at the total figure you are projecting in sales from these yet-to-be clients. Now, consider what mix of products/ services you project you'll sell into each of these accounts, and for what revenue/margin. Be conservative — don't project every new sale at the levels of the largest new sale you've ever made. Be realistic. Once you've worked this out, divide the value of your average new sale into your total target to get the number of new clients you're going to need to come in to finish on forecast. Great — now you have a clear picture of your targets for new client numbers, product mix and revenue/margin figures. Hold those thoughts.

Before Question 2, let's take some time to look at your sales cycle. For the purposes of this discussion, we're going to assume that you get your business from quotations or proposals; that these proposals/quotations come about as a result of one or a series of one-to-one meetings and/or presentations; that your one-to-ones come as a result of initial appointments generated from lead-generation activity; and that your main means of lead generation are either cold calls or mailshot-driven 'warm calls'. If your deal cycle is different, then simply apply the thinking we're going to explore to the milestones that characterise your typical sale.

From Question 1 you know how many new deals you need to close to hit the new business figure for this year. What are you doing today, and every day, about getting them? If you're not investing in enough focused activity, then, regardless of how desirable or possible the result you've projected, you just won't hit your numbers. But how can you tell if you're involved in enough of the right activity to assure your success? That's the focus of Question 2.

Question 2: What's Your Proposal Hit Rate?

Before you can determine the likely effectiveness of your activity plan, you're going to have to do some spadework — digging into your past experience of your typical sales cycle to fine-tune your forecast. From your previous experience, the first thing you'll need to estimate is how many proposals you're going to have to produce to hit the number of deals you've forecast. Look at what happened last year, and at what's happened so far this year. If you don't have useful previous performance figures to draw upon, then estimate very, very conservatively — err on the side of more rather than fewer proposals. Let's say you get a 1-in-3 hit rate with your proposals, then, to close 10 deals, you're going to need requests for 30 proposals.

Question 3: How Many Meetings to Get to Proposal?

Now, these proposals resulted from one or a series of meetings/presentations and selling activity. What does your previous performance tell you about the number of prospects you need to engage in one or a series of one-to-ones to get one prospect to proposal stage? In other words, how many brand new suspects do you have to meet before you find one that has an identifiable need for what you offer and the budget/wherewithal/willingness to go down the proposal route with you? Again, conservative realism is key. Let's say that one in two of all new contacts you ever meet results in a request for proposal, then your target of 30 proposals demands that you meet at least sixty new people to hit your forecast.

Step 4: How Many Calls to Get a Meeting?

We assumed that you won these meetings from targeted cold or warm calls to suspects identified from your research or list. How many calls will you need to make? Let's say you have a 1-in-4 hit rate on converting calls to appointments, then, to get 60 appointments, you are going to need to target and speak with 240 new prospects. Finally, let's say it takes an average of four calls to get each of your target suspects on the telephone after you've mailed them, then you've 960 calls to make this year.

So, in our example, your modest target of ten new deals demands that you:

- Make 960 calls to speak with 240 new people…

- to get meetings with 60 of them…

- to get to proposal with 30 of them…

- and to close 10 of them.

When you work out this breakdown of your own forecast, it will tell you a whole lot about the reality of your forecast.

If this were your forecast, then, assuming an even spread of activity over a 250-day business year, you'd need to be making about 20 calls to new people per week; meeting a new suspect every four days; dispatching a proposal about every eight business days; and closing a deal every five weeks. These hard measures are the only objective means to determine how realistic your forecast is.

So, given where you are right now, how are you doing? Are you hitting your call, meeting, proposal, close targets so far this year? Be honest with yourself — and, if you're not meeting those targets, then it's back to the drawing board.

Sometimes, an in-depth look at your forecast in this manner will tell you in no uncertain terms that you simply don't have the time or resources to undertake the necessary activity. If the activity level required to hit your numbers is simply impossible, given other commitments like existing account selling, implementation, servicing or any other responsibilities you might have, then you cannot hit your forecast numbers without changing something. Either reorganise and resource yourself so that you hit these key activity milestones, or recalibrate where your business is going to come from, and do it **now**!

If it's obvious that you won't be able to hit your originally forecasted numbers, do something about any mis-projection now. You'll never have more of your year left than you do today!

> *You must know: How many proposals to get one sale? How many meetings to get to a proposal? How many calls to get a meeting?*

This examination might also tell you that your estimates in terms of call–one-to-one–proposal–close conversion rates were overly optimistic, and that to hit your numbers you're going to have to ramp your activity up even further.

There are other issues that this analysis will also force you to face. For example, how long is the cycle from first meeting to proposal? If, in the example above, we were working with a lead time of six months from initial contact to doing business, even meeting all of the activity targets you've calculated will not bring the required level of business in on time. In that case, you'd have to increase the number of people out chasing deals, find another source of income, or cut your forecast back.

The message is simple — take a hard look at your forecast for new business, and reduce it using a set of SMART (*Specific, Measurable, Achievable, Realistic, Timebound*) activity/ result milestones that allow you to determine whether you are on or off target.

Make your forecast a living tool that ensures your success by comparing your actual progress against each of these milestones on a daily, weekly, monthly and quarterly basis — and adjust your course if you start to slide off target.

Success or failure in sales does not happen by accident — the future is entirely in your hands.

Strategy 25

Back to the Future

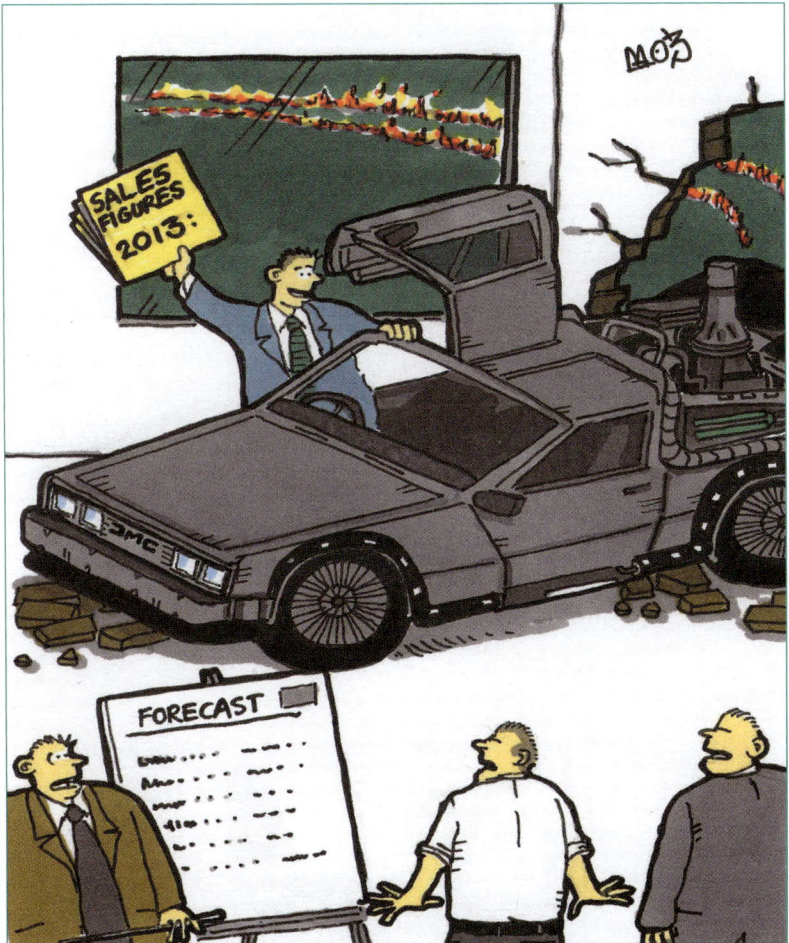

Back to the Future

How Much is Your
Pipeline Really Worth?

Ever wondered how you manage to miss your sales targets despite the fact that you always seem to have more than enough business on the go any time you look?

In Strategy 24, we looked at how you plan enough of the right activity to ensure that you have a fighting chance of hitting the aggressive sales targets you set yourself in Quarter 1. Now we look at how you manage the prospects that result from this ongoing activity — to ensure that you have enough potential business live at any time to keep you on your weekly, monthly and quarterly targets right to the end of a successful year.

To do this, you'll need to take three steps to establish structured forecasts that will operate as your early-warning system any time you begin to veer off target.

Step 1. Look at Your Deal Cycle

Map out your typical sales cycle and estimate how close each step in that cycle takes you to issuing an invoice. For example, let's say that in our business we find that we must meet fifty new people to get to proposal stage with just twenty of them. Ten of these proposals will be given a positive reception when we present them, and, of these ten, we find that we eventually get a verbal 'Yes!' from six. Sadly, one of these six verbal go-aheads will fail to become new business — but at least we end up with five deals. The probability of closing a deal at each of the key points in our deal cycle is therefore:

First Meeting: *10% (5 in 50 become business)*
Issue Proposal: *25% (5 in 20 become business)*
Positive Proposal Presentation *50% (5 in 10 become business)*
Verbal 'Yes'   *80%+ (5 in 6 become business)*
Signed Contract   *100% (5 in 5 become business)*

If you don't have historical data to estimate conversion rates at each stage, start collecting that data for future use, and, in the meantime, estimate working percentages cautiously.

Step 2. Estimate the Real Value of Your Prospect List

The next step is to work out exactly how much the prospective sales you are currently working on are really worth. After all, regardless of how good you are, some of these deals will close, and some will drop out at various points in the cycle. Table 1 looks at how you can calculate the Real Value of your current prospects.

TABLE 1

Prospect	Potential Value	Probability	Real Value	Close Month
Profiles Ltd	€20,000	25%	€4,000	June
Strategy Ltd	€15,000	50%	€7,500	May
ClientCo Ltd	€10,000	80%	€8,000	April
Total Forecast			**€19,500**	

Table 1

From the discussion in Step 1, we know that when we issue four proposals, we end up with at least one deal; so any one proposal is worth just 25 per cent of its potential value. So, having issued Profiles with a proposal, we estimate its current *Real Value* as 25 per cent of the total €20,000 of the proposal. With Strategy Ltd, we've had a positive reaction to our proposal presentation, and as we know that we tend to close about half of the deals that get to this stage, we've calculated its *Real Value* as 50 per cent of the proposal value. Finally, ClientCo Ltd. has said 'Yes', but we're still awaiting a formal contract — we know that we lose one in six of the deals that get to this stage so the value of that deal is just 80 per cent of the proposal's value — it won't become a certain billing opportunity until we get a signed contract. So, while there is potential for as much as €45K worth of business in our pipeline, the *Real Value* of our forecasted sales is just a fraction of this.

If your target for Quarter 2 was €30K, and the table above was your Quarter-2 forecast, then, before your analysis, you might have relaxed on the basis that you had 1.5 times your target in the pipeline. However, you now know that the total forecast has a Real Value that falls well short of your target for the quarter — so you're going to have to get a few more deals on the go to ensure that you will hit your numbers.

To manage your sales pipeline effectively, this analysis must be undertaken on a rolling basis — providing you with a

view of the future that informs the activity you must be engaged in here in the present.

Step 3. Look at Your Timescales

The rightmost column of Table 1 contains that information on your forecast that is frequently most difficult to get right — the estimated timing of the deal close. Both salespeople and clients tend to positively over-estimate how quickly they'll get to a 'yes'. If in doubt, be cautious. When you get this element correct, your forecast becomes even more useful. Now, you can reorganise your analysis in the manner of Table 2.

Be honest: how much is your forecasted business worth in real terms?

TABLE 2

Prospect	April	May	June
Profiles Ltd	—	—	€4,000
Strategy Ltd	—	€7,500	—
ClientCo Ltd	€8,000	—	—
Totals	**€8,000**	**€7,500**	**€4,000**

Table 2

This analysis gives you a clear view of the trends that will affect your sales over the coming months. In the example, it is clear that sales are tailing off over the three months of Quarter 2. So, if you're to remedy this slippage, it's clear that some of the activity that you scheduled using the approach discussed in the previous strategy may have to be accelerated or brought forward if your sales are not to disappear altogether by Quarter 3.

Ongoing analysis like this will provide you with all of the information you need to ensure achievement of even the most aggressive sales targets.

Open up your own window on the future today and eliminate the element of chance from achievement of even the most aggressive sales targets.

Strategy 26

Sales Doctor

Sales Doctor

What Ails your Sales?

Are you selling as much as you should? Sales are the life's blood of every organisation — without sales, we wither and die. If you or one of your salespeople goes off track, use this systematic diagnosis to identify where you need to focus your time, money and effort to put things back on track.

What Causes Low Sales?

As illustrated by the *Sales Doctor* flowchart, there are two basic problems. Either you're not getting in front of enough people or, when you do, you're not getting as far as 'yes!' Which is it in your situation? Be honest, and go to either '*1. Too Few Presentations*' or '*2. Not Closing*' below.

1. Too Few Presentations

There are two main reasons why salespeople don't get enough one-to-one meetings. Is your problem that you *1a. Can't Generate Enough Prospects?* Or could you potentially get enough prospects but have problems with *1c. Poor Time Management*, and therefore cannot get face-to-face with enough of them? Decide where your stumbling block lies and then read on from that point.

SALES DOCTOR *FLOWCHART*

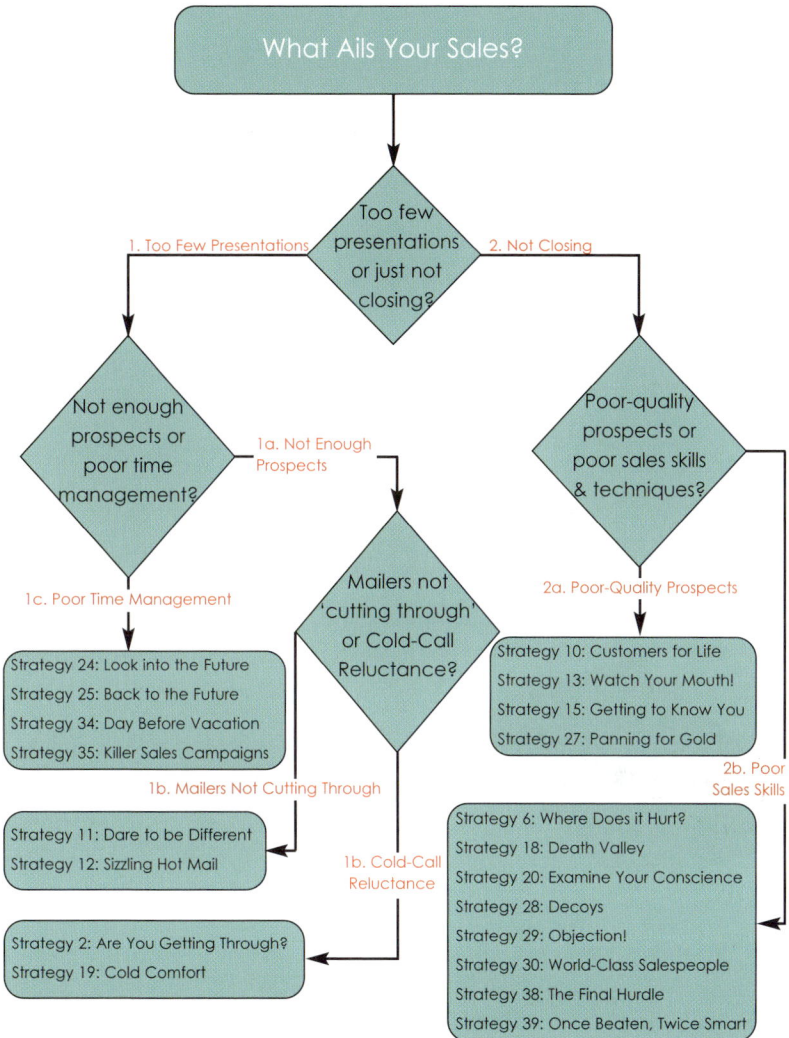

What Ails Your Sales?

1. Too Few Presentations — Too few presentations or just not closing? — 2. Not Closing

Not enough prospects or poor time management?

1a. Not Enough Prospects

Poor-quality prospects or poor sales skills & techniques?

1c. Poor Time Management

Mailers not 'cutting through' or Cold-Call Reluctance?

2a. Poor-Quality Prospects

Strategy 24: Look into the Future
Strategy 25: Back to the Future
Strategy 34: Day Before Vacation
Strategy 35: Killer Sales Campaigns

Strategy 10: Customers for Life
Strategy 13: Watch Your Mouth!
Strategy 15: Getting to Know You
Strategy 27: Panning for Gold

2b. Poor Sales Skills

1b. Mailers Not Cutting Through

Strategy 11: Dare to be Different
Strategy 12: Sizzling Hot Mail

1b. Cold-Call Reluctance

Strategy 6: Where Does it Hurt?
Strategy 18: Death Valley
Strategy 20: Examine Your Conscience
Strategy 28: Decoys
Strategy 29: Objection!
Strategy 30: World-Class Salespeople
Strategy 38: The Final Hurdle
Strategy 39: Once Beaten, Twice Smart

Strategy 2: Are You Getting Through?
Strategy 19: Cold Comfort

1a. Can't Generate Enough Prospects

If the problem is one of a prospect drought, you need to act urgently — once your prospect pipeline dries up, you are living on borrowed time. Look at your sales targets and determine how many units of your products or services you need to sell to make target. Then, from your experience, determine how many proposals it takes to get a sale, how many meetings to get to a proposal, and how many telephone conversations or mailers you need to get a meeting. Divide these activity targets by the selling days in your business year. If you haven't created and implemented a solid plan to hit each of these activity targets reliably, you haven't a hope. Get your plan in place now.

Strategies 24: Look into the Future, 25: Back to the Future, and 35: Killer Sales Campaigns offer solid step-by-step processes for effective sales planning and forecasting.

If prospect activity levels are not your problem, consider other problems like *1b. Mailer Cut-Through & Cold-Call Reluctance* or *2b. Poor Sales Skills & Techniques*.

1b.Mailer Cut-Through & Cold-Call Reluctance

Assuming that you have a tight prospecting activity plan, and that you know whom you need to target with what, but that you still have problems with too few prospects, then, either:

- Your mailers are not 'cutting through', or

- You could be suffering from Cold-Call Reluctance.

Mailer 'Cut-Through'
The volume of junk mail we all have to deal with rises daily and, unless your mailer is good enough, all of your effort goes straight in the bin. Don't panic — there's help at hand. Look at the *Sales Doctor* flowchart for advice on three strategies

that can help you to turn all of your mailers into 'sizzlers' that cut through to your prospect's attention every time.

Cold-Call Reluctance

If your mailers are fine, but the follow-up a little slow, you may be suffering from the most persistent and corrosive of sales problems — *Cold-Call Reluctance*. Every salesperson has been afflicted with it at some time or other (regardless of what they might tell you!) Cold-Call Reluctance is exactly what it sounds like — a difficulty in picking up the phone to ask for an appointment or sale. All of the research in this area shows that call reluctance is fundamentally rooted in the fear of failure that sometimes afflicts those whose jobs involve persuasion. It can be addressed with training, coaching, and support. But before rushing into training expense, check out the *Sales Doctor* flowchart for two great strategies that address this sales killer.

> *Cold-Call Reluctance is a normal part of life for anyone involved in selling — and it's manageable.*

1c. Poor Time Management

Some people are naturals when it comes to making the most of this basic resource — the rest of us have to use structured systems. Successful salespeople use systems for both advanced sales planning and day-to-day time management.

The *Sales Doctor* flowchart suggests three great strategies that can help you out with sales planning and forecasting — getting the 'big picture' right.

175

Your only remaining challenge is to manage your day-to-day activities to ensure that you execute your plan effectively. If you are not a natural time manager, invest in good-quality training from one of the many masters in this area — Time Manager and Priority Manager are just two of the many quality training organisations working in this area.

2. Not Closing

Why do you sometimes fail to close after spending so much time to get in front of a prospect? Decide if it's *2a. Poor-Quality Prospects* or *2b. Poor Sales Skills & Techniques*, and then skip to that point and continue reading.

2a. Poor-Quality Prospects

Failure to identify and target appropriate prospects is one of the most basic sales ailments. There are four strategies that can help you greatly in these key areas. Check out the *Sales Doctor* flowchart to see which ones you need most.

2b. Poor Sales Skills & Techniques

So you're making lots of appointments with good-quality prospects but still not managing to bring in sales?

If you don't have a clear structure to guide you from first contact through analysis of client requirements and identification of benefits to a clean deal close, you need to fix that now.

The *Sales Doctor* flowchart provides you with eight meaty strategies which offer powerful and practical advice on these key sales skills.

The moment you see your sales start to suffer, Doc, use the *Sales Doctor* flowchart to diagnose the problem precisely and address it before it becomes an epidemic that wipes you out.

Strategy 27

Panning for Gold

Panning for Gold

Prospecting is a Lot Like Panning for Gold

Prospecting for new customers is a lot like panning for gold. Know what you're looking for, look in the right place, use the right tools and techniques, and you'll get gold; otherwise all you get is a useless pile of well-sifted dirt.

It's hard to believe people who tell you that they enjoy prospecting. Prospecting is a tough, time-consuming, and often boringly repetitive activity, fraught with ego-crushing rejection. But it's necessary. If you've a six-month sales cycle, you made the opportunity for today's sale six months ago. So your sales six months from now are entirely dependent on what you do today. Prospecting must be part of your everyday activities.

What most prospectors often miss is that the success of a prospecting campaign is determined BEFORE it begins. Two preparatory steps are vital.

Step 1. Develop a Formal Profile of your Ideal Customer

Forget about who you would like to be your ideal customer, or who your marketing or product people say are the ideal customers for your products or services. Look at who is actually buying from you, and who is buying from your closest competitors. Who are they? What size are they? When do they buy? Why do they buy? Draw up a formal profile of those customers — because it's more of them that you want to uncover when you go prospecting. Summarise the profile so that you can recite it in thirty seconds or less — and be sure that everyone in your organisation is equally familiar with it.

Step 2. Develop a 'Why Us?' Statement

Prospects must have compelling reasons to buy from you. Develop a statement summarising all of those reasons. In developing this statement, think: What's so special about what I offer? How are my offerings superior to everyone else's? Who are my most impressive customers and why did they buy from me? What are my offerings' disadvantages and how can I overcome them? Don't trust yourself — ask your best customers why they bought from you; and listen carefully. Use this input to produce a conversational 30-second statement summarising all of the reasons why prospects should buy from you. Refine it by reciting it to colleagues. When it's perfect, be sure that everyone who has contact with your customer or prospect base can produce it as required.

Look carefully at the types of customers who are buying from you — know them inside out.

179

With a profile of your ideal customer, and knowing why they should buy from you, you are ready to start prospecting. Only then. Here are some guidelines that will make your prospecting activity less time-consuming and more productive.

Recognise that Prospecting is Not Selling per se

...it is relationship building — creating an environment where a prospect wants to become a customer. Focus on the relationship — think of their needs, not yours. When the relationship is established, the sales follow.

Keep Close to Existing Customers

Take proper care of existing customers and they're the easiest prospecting territory. Understand your sales cycle and be alert to when they should be repurchasing, upgrading or replacing. In larger accounts, prospect in new areas, using your knowledge of their business as a door-opener.

Every Time You Sell, Look for Referrals

New customers are as positive about you as they'll ever be just after you've sold to them. Ask for referrals at the moment of sale. If they can't point you at anyone specific, find out from them where folks in their industry get their information from — what associations they belong to, what magazines they read, what conferences they attend. Others like them will flock there.

180

Make Sure You're Visible to Likely Prospects

Find out what industry journals your prospects read and look at what they publish. Submit your own articles. Be sure that you know who organises any regular industry conferences or events, and get yourself on speakers' lists. Make yourself a visible authority in your prospects' industries.

Network

Attend any forum, conference, exhibition or event where you know that your prospects will congregate. Talk to as many people as you can. Deliver your 'Why us?' statement, exchange business cards, and move on.

> *Prospecting is relationship building — creating an environment where a prospect wants to become a customer.*

Extend Your Reach

Lift a rock in your garden and you'll see lots of insects swarming around in an incredibly small area. All of them are make a living — because many of them don't compete for the same food or homestead. Your prospecting territory is like that — there are many non-competing organisations chasing your customers and prospects for business. Seek them out and build relationships with them — you pass them leads, and they pass you leads. Simple, but effective.

DO Take No for an Answer

Forget all that sales twaddle about the challenge to the salesperson of a 'No!' The real challenge is to resist trying to turn every 'No!' around, recognising when 'no' really means 'No!' If in doubt, qualify out. Quickly. If a prospect hasn't a compelling reason to buy from you, find one who does. Selling time, energy and resources are much too valuable, and there are always lots more prospects who are worthy of your efforts.

Don't Worry about Failing

Prospecting is a numbers game. However successful your campaign, you'll have mis-hits. Learn from them. Think of Thomas Edison when his inventions repeatedly failed to perform as he expected: '*I didn't fail a thousand times, I learned a thousand ways it wouldn't work.*'

There's gold in them thar hills! Go get it.

Strategy 28

Decoys

Decoys

Is it the 'Real Deal'?

Time is money, and the most annoying waste of that money for a hard-pushed salesperson is on the pursuit of business that you were never going to win in the first place — because it wasn't real. As salespeople, we are continually faced with the problem of *Decoy* opportunities — apparent opportunities that are fabricated for a variety of reasons.

The sad truth is that you will occasionally receive a Request For Proposal (RFP) from clients or consultants, requesting that you bid for supply of products or services which they have no intention whatever of purchasing. The good news is that you don't have to be a victim — not if you take the time to review every opportunity that comes your way to ensure that it is not one of these *Decoy* opportunities.

Why are *Decoys* Used?

Decoy RFPs are released for a great variety of reasons, the most common being:

- Research/Free Consultation/Information
  Sometimes an RFP is issued by a client or a consultant who wants nothing more than to develop a view of the current state of developments in a given industry.

184

Experience suggests that many consultants find the proposal process a very useful way to conduct basic research on behalf of their clients — research for which they get paid.

However, you obviously can't refuse to deal with any consultant or client who may approach you, simply on the basis of such experience. What if the consultant who approaches you is genuinely trying to find a solution to a particular client problem? Well, it's a judgement call. If the consultant is known to you personally or has clearly done a lot of work in preparing a convincing RFP or briefing document, or if you are invited to meet the client personally, you may feel comfortable with the situation. If, however, you have any reservations, qualify carefully and don't be afraid to walk away — to spend your time on opportunities of which you are more certain. Qualify out early — on the simple basis that you will likely get a better return on your time pursuing other opportunities.

> Sometimes proposals are requested for reasons other than a desire to purchase — don't be a Decoy victim.

● To Prepare a More Comprehensive RFP

A vague RFP, one in which there has been little time invested, from a substantial client, for an obviously genuine requirement can often signal that the client is looking to produce a more comprehensive RFP from a

combination of all of the best aspects of any proposals submitted (it can also signal the opportunity of your life — so don't be too cynical). If you suspect that this is the case, you must decide whether or not the client is worth the effort — you must weigh up whether you are prepared to give away your best ideas against the obvious benefits to having some input into the final RFP document.

- ## To Build a Specification for an In-house Project
  This is perhaps the most cynical use of the proposal process — and it is not at all uncommon. The client prepares a comprehensive RFP document and solicits a number of very detailed responses and follow-up presentations. Very often, the decision to proceed is then put 'on hold' during the evaluation process.

  All we can say on this one is that the type of organisation that pursues this sort of policy very often fits the 'repeat offenders' category. So, 'Once bitten, twice shy.'

How Do You Spot a Decoy?

There is no definitive way to spot a Decoy RFP, but they generally have one or more of the following characteristics:

- ## The Bluebird
  Every so often, every salesperson is lucky enough to get a 'Bluebird' — a deal which comes 'right out of the blue', never having appeared on any account plan or revenue projections, only to position itself to become the year's big earner.

A *Decoy* RFP is almost always a Bluebird. Watch out for them.

- **Non-Client**

  Decoy RFPs will very often come from an organisation which is not currently a client — very often a prospect which you have been trying to break into for some time.

- **Size**

  In order to cause an instant brain shutdown, to disable your normally very sharp qualification faculties, the *Decoy* prospect will very often be large and the opportunity substantial. Think — why are they suddenly contacting you now?

- **Short Timescale**

  This is a high-value, strategic acquisition, yet the decision will be made on what seems to be an almost impossibly short timescale and your response is required on an unreasonably short timescale.

- **Little on Paper**

  A *Decoy* RFP will quite often betray itself by the lack of effort invested in its preparation. The RFP will very often be high level, giving little detail on the supposed requirement.

Large-scale deals that suddenly pop up on your radar, with short response timescales and little information are often Decoys. Seller beware!

187

- ### Detail

  Despite its own non-detailed nature, the *Decoy* RFP will usually require a great amount of detail on your products, services and costs.

- ### Limited Contact within the Prospect

  A tell-tale sign of a *Decoy* RFP is the level of contact you are afforded within the prospect organisation. If the requirement is so substantial, the value so large, and the timescale so tight, how come there are so few of the prospect's senior managers involved in the acquisition?

Don't Be a *Decoy* Victim

Unless you see some particular benefit to proceeding with a proposal to meet an opportunity that you feel sure is a *Decoy* (building your profile within a strategic account, for example), then, in general, we suggest that you run away — save your energies for those opportunities you are satisfied you have a real chance to convert into revenue.

Whatever you do, when you find yourself in pursuit of an opportunity that is, in fact, a *Decoy*, be sure it's for your reasons, that you have made the conscious decision to follow this course — that no one else is pulling the strings.

Strategy 29

Objection!

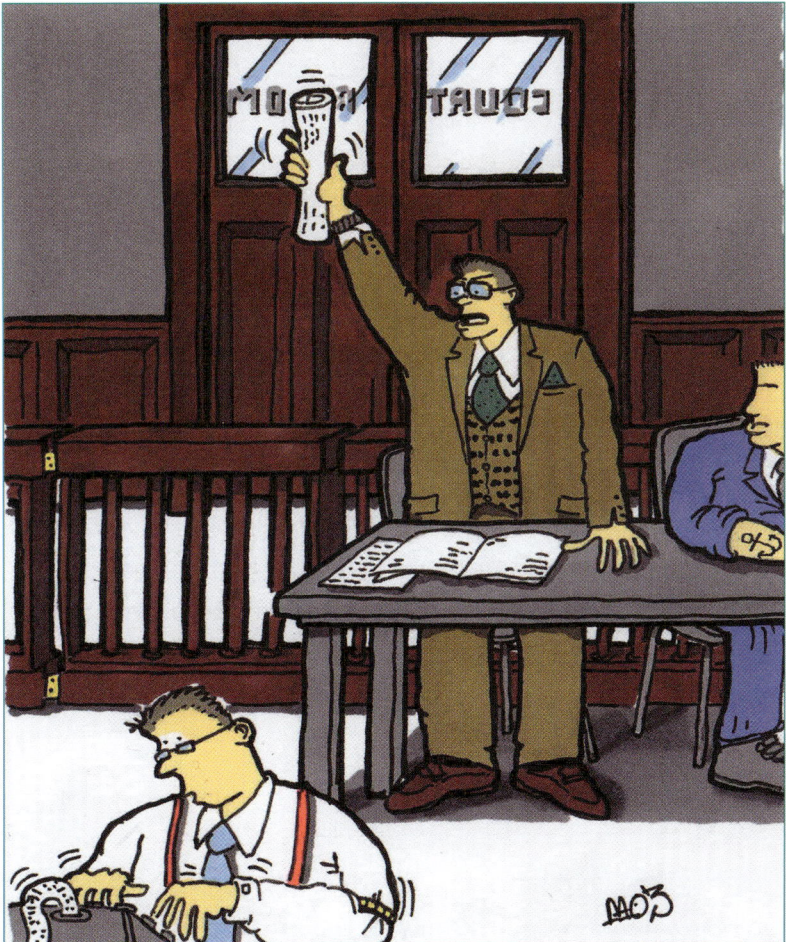

Objection!

What to Say
When They Say, 'No!'

In just about every business today, competition is such that selection of suppliers is done on the basis of a formal proposal process — where purchasers outline their requirements and invite prospective suppliers to 'bid' for their business.

A winning proposal is based on the basic six-part model: Executive Summary — Your Requirement — Our Solution to Your Requirement — Benefits of our Proposed Solution — Costs — Appendices. Assuming that you have used this winning framework, there is still a lot of edge to be gained over your competition by requesting that your client allow you to present the content of your proposal. After all, we all know that few clients will read every word in our proposals, and the ones they miss may well be the ones that set you apart from your competitors. A face-to-face presentation is an ideal opportunity to drive home the particularly positive points of your proposal.

Be Sure to Expect Objections

Once your client has agreed to your presenting a summary of the content of your proposal, you are faced with the fact that, in every proposal presentation you make, your audience will raise some sort of objection. An objection can be your audience's way of indicating that they are seriously interested in what you have to say, but that they need more information on certain points in order to accept your arguments. Objections can also indicate, however, that the client is totally disinterested in what you have to say, and that they are simply looking for a way to say 'no'.

When you are preparing, reviewing or rehearsing your presentation, take a note of any point at all to which your client could possibly raise any sort of objection. Be sure that you have included every objection you can conceive of. Don't just rely on your own judgement in this — ask other members of the team to identify any points on which they feel the client might base an objection.

> An objection can be your audience's way of saying, 'I need more information.'

When you have what you feel to be a comprehensive list of likely objections, develop positive responses to them. If any of the objections are technical in nature, either be sure that you assimilate sufficient knowledge to be able to handle the objection yourself, or plan to invite one of your more technical colleagues who will support you at the presentation, to address the objection.

Handling Objections

If you have prepared adequately, you will be ready to address the majority of the objections raised. So, when they are raised, how do you handle them? Follow the five-step approach outlined below:

Step 1. Do and Say Nothing (for a moment)

Be seen to listen intently to the objection, nodding your head in understanding, and then to think for a moment, considering the objection — saying nothing. There are two values to this momentary silence. In the first instance, it indicates that you are truly thinking about the objection, that your response is not just one of a set of glib, rehearsed responses. Secondly, this momentary silence will very often prompt the questioner, or another audience member, to expand upon their objection, even to the extent of indicating what they think your response should be.

Step 2. Confirm Your Understanding of the Objection

To further drive home the impression that you are truly considering the objection, and to ensure that your understanding of the objection is correct, you should confirm your understanding of the objection. Do this by paraphrasing the objection and presenting it back to the client in an '*Am I correct that your concern is...?*' or '*If I understand you correctly, you are concerned that...*' form. Never attempt to address an objection until you have qualified it as valid.

Step 3. Respond to the Objection Confidently and Authoritatively

Deliver your prepared response in a confident and authoritative tone. If the objection was one which you had not anticipated, either formulate a reasonable response there and then or, if it would be more effective, offer to research the objection later and to return to the client with a response. In this instance, be seen to note this objection carefully for later action.

Step 4. Confirm that Your Response has Satisfactorily Addressed the Objection

'Does this answer your concern on...?' If not, then return to Step 2 and re-state the objection, or a new definition of the particular aspect of the objection that you have failed to address.

Step 5. Return to Where You Were in Your Presentation

One of the most important aspects of having prepared for objections is your ability to handle them, and still be able to return to the point to which your presentation had pro-gressed before the interruption.

> Take a few moments in silence after you've heard the objection — more information often emerges to fill the gap.

What if You Can't Agree?

If you do feel that you have addressed the objection, but the client does not concur, avoid arguing the point with the client — you can't win. Offer to research the objection fur-ther, and pointedly note the objection. Put as positive a face as you can on your response and move on.

What if You Have No Good Response?

If the client introduces an objection for which you have no good response, try to present an equally positive aspect of your proposed solution that might help to offset the negative impact of the objection. For example, '... *Yes, MyCorp's solution is 20 per cent more expensive than that of our next nearest competitor, but independent research has shown that the life of our product is 40 per cent longer than that of the next nearest in the marketplace, and we are acknowledged as the market leader in ongoing support.*'

Key Points in Objection Handling

- View every objection positively — they are all opportunities to drive home the positive benefits of your proposal.

- Be very careful not to be seen to be defensive in responding to objections.

- Be enthusiastic about your company, and its products and services — regardless of what objections are raised. Don't accept negative comments about you, your company, or your products or services, without some positive counteractive response.

- Don't lie or exaggerate. If you don't have a ready answer, say so — committing to return with a response at a later date.

- The client is always right — even when they're wrong. Don't argue with the audience; don't tell them they're wrong; try not to get hung up on individuals' personalities.

The key to getting past objections is simple: don't ever give up. However poorly you feel that you are answering the client's objections, your competitors' responses may well be even less effective.

Stay in the game till the end.

Strategy 30

World-Class Salespeople

World-Class Salespeople

Spotting the 20% who Sell the 80%

When Vilfredo Pareto formulated his famous 80–20 rule in 1900, could he have guessed that 100 years later, his rule would apply to sales in organisations like yours — with about 20 per cent of all salespeople making 80 per cent of all sales?

Research consistently demonstrates that over half of those in professional sales lack the basic attributes required for success in this difficult profession — attributes that World-Class Salespeople possess as natural gifts or develop through training or single-minded focus. Of the remaining half, half of these again have the potential for success in some form of sales, but are currently selling the wrong product or service — leaving just about 25 per cent who sell about 80 per cent of the world's products and services. Scary.

That's why it is so key that all those of us with responsibility for driving our businesses forward have a keen understanding of the attributes that make for World-Class Salespeople — so that we can hire more of them. It's also key if we are to recognise where any struggling salespeople on our team might need training or support.

Run all of your salespeople against this list of the ten attributes that World-Class Salespeople share in common:

(I) Irrepressibly Positive Attitude

All of their glasses are half-full and every cloud they encounter has a silver lining. Knock them down nine times and they stand up ten. Without this iron optimism, a life in sales is a stressful and daunting existence.

Do your sales heroes live in a partly cloudy or partly sunny world?

(II) Understand that Sales is a Numbers Game

They don't lose their cool when a call goes badly, a deal goes south, or a first contact ends in refusal — they simply focus more carefully on the next call. They know their hit rate from

25% of all salespeople sell 80% of all products sold. Scary!

past experience — they know how often they'll have to take 'No!' on the chin to get to one 'Yes'.

Do your salespeople know the value of their calls?

(III) Live to Prospect

The World-Class Salespeople are prospecting all of the time — especially when things are going so well that everyone else has stopped. They know that sales success is directly dependent upon continually filling their pipelines with well-qualified prospects. Prospecting is their obsession — they never stop.

Is prospecting 24 / 7 / 365 in your organisation?

(IV) Totally Sales-Driven

These people live for the chase that results in a closed deal; they are internally motivated to go to whatever lengths they must to win the business. They seem to have unceasing energy — once they decide to do something, once they get the bit between their teeth, nothing slows or stops them until they have succeeded.

Are your salespeople in top gear?

(V) Competitive

The need to win informs everything else that they do. They don't like second, and they are not good losers. Sure, they know that they must affect a 'good-loser' performance from time to time — for social reasons. But deep down, they need to win, and losses just stiffen their resolve. They can't be kept to second place for long.

*Is your team **too** good at losing?*

(VI) Obsessed with the 'Next Step'

Everything they do is about getting to the 'next step', about getting the next level of commitment that brings the client ever closer to the level of trust and confidence needed for a 'Yes!' World-Class Salespeople think solely in terms of specifics like 'where', 'when', 'how', 'how much'. Woolly concepts like 'sometime', 'in the future', 'later', 'whenever' are simply not in their vocabularies. The most successful salespeople in Profiles International know that their success is inevitable, but they still drive to 'accelerate the inevitable'.

Are your salespeople driving their case forward at least one step with every client or prospect contact?

(VII) Know that They and Their Products are World Class

Quiet confidence oozes out of top salespeople, and un-bridled enthusiasm for their company and products/services gushes from them at everyone they meet. No one is left untouched by the passion they pull upon when they talk about themselves, their companies, or their products and services. They evangelise.

Have your people been to the top of the mountain?

(VIII) Qualify Hard before Investing Time and Energy

Time is too precious to waste on people who don't have the need for what they can provide. They understand their products and services inside out, understand the needs they address, understand why their offerings are so much better than those of their competitors, and know enough about their prospective clients that they rarely find themselves in front of someone who is not a genuine prospective client.

World-Class Salespeople are obsessed with the next step.

Do your salespeople look before they leap?

(IX) Expect to Hear 'No!'

Once they know that they are in front of the right people, these champions are confident that they have considered every possible 'No!' situation that might arise, and they understand how to address these objections in a way that builds the confidence and trust of their prospective clients.

Are your front people always ready to handle key objections?

(X) Sell through Client Knowledge

Ask clients of World-Class Salespeople what sets them apart and they'll tell you, 'They understand us.' These people never stop trying to ferret out more information about the client and their needs — they know that the only way they can deliver sales that become valuable relationships is through partnership and problem-solving.

How much do your salespeople know about their clients and prospects?

When you hire new salespeople, you must look for these key attributes. Now, that's sometimes easier said than done — just how do you objectively measure these attributes in someone whose career is built around selling their prospects the ideal view of what they have to offer?

Effectively Spot the 20%

That's a challenge we faced in building our 800-strong worldwide sales force in Profiles International — and we met it head on with the development of the *Profiles Sales Indicator (PSI)*.

First the *PSI* analyses your existing salespeople to produce a profile of what it takes to be a successful salesperson in your organisation. Then, using your prospective sales-person's responses to a 15–20-minute online survey, the *PSI* objectively analyses the extent to which that person has five key attributes:

- Competitiveness

- Self-reliance

- Persistence

- Energy

- Sales Drive.

By comparing these results with the profile of your most successful salespeople, *PSI* can then predict on-the-job performance in seven critical sales disciplines:

- Prospecting

- Closing Sales

- Call Reluctance

- Self-starting

- Teamwork

- Building and Maintaining Relationships

- Compensation Preference

— all of the areas essential to the success of the top-performing 20 per cent of salespeople responsible for 80 per cent of all sales.

The *PSI*'s clear, readable reports can be used for selecting new salespeople, or for more effective management and training of existing salespeople to ensure that they reach the performance levels of your top performers.

The *Sales Indicator* worked so well for Profiles International that we have now made it available to all. You can read more about it on the web at:

www.profilesinternational.com

Take action today to move all of your team into the 20 per cent zone, and watch your sales soar.

Strategy 31

The Sky is Not Falling

The Sky is Not Falling

Good Tactics for Bad Times

Tough times turn a larger-than-normal percentage of the business population into latter-day Chicken Littles — all running around, shouting frenzied proclamations of the end of the commercial world as we know it.

If you're a guilty part of this *fowl* movement, STOP! STOP NOW! before you contribute to this potentially self-fulfilling doomsday prophesying. I quizzed one of our suppliers — a one-man band — on his prediction as to the likely future effect of a previous downturn on his business and got a simple answer: 'None! because I'm not taking part in it!' Of course, that's pretty much impossible, right?

Wrong — what he has is the correct *attitude* — you can always ride tough times out if you work a little harder and determine that you'll minimise any adverse impact on sales. But how?

Here are ten tactics for coping in tough times — all of which your sales organisation can quickly action. Some of these actions are specifically aimed at sales-management level; others at every salesperson in the organisation. To maximise your chances of success, you need to implement every one of them to help you to balance out the negative effects that weakened consumer confidence can have on your sales volume in tighter times.

1. Cross- and Up-Sell in Existing Active Accounts

Active purchasers/users of your products and services who are buying from you currently may have a need for something else that you do — and you don't yet know (and neither do they, likely as not). Get out and find out. Look at ways of up-selling and cross-selling into all of these accounts. How could they blend one service/product they currently use with another they've never used? What would be the benefit to them of doing so? What financial/other incentive can you give them to do so? Think about it first; then formulate as many cross- and up-sell strategies as you can for everything that you currently provide. Look at packaging sets of goods and services to have an impact, so that you add value and revenue to every single sale you make. With a little imagination, you'll find that you can up the value of every sale, and create brand new sales, with little additional sales effort. It doesn't have to result in a doubling of the

> Downturns can't affect your business if you refuse to take part in them! It's all about attitude.

value of every sale you make, or in doubling the take from every one of your existing accounts. Even modest margin increases on every sale you make will add up substantially over time. Look at how McDonald's and Burger King approach every one of their admittedly individually modest sales — '*Would you like fries with that?*' or '*Would you like to go large?*' Do it now — talk to all customers currently buying from you and seek to up the value of every sale into every one of those accounts, one way or another. Go large!

2. Awaken Hibernating Accounts

Review the records of everyone you've ever done business with — you'll find that there are some on that list who, for whatever reason, have had no contact from you or your sales force for some time. Good times are like that — we all tend to chase the 'low-hanging fruit' — the opportunities that walk up to us and say, 'Take me!' There will be some clients who have had excellent experience with you, but who haven't done anything with you recently because you simply didn't ask. Get out and see everyone. Things have changed since you saw them last — for one thing, you're much hungrier and, if you've actioned the first point above, you now have so many 'packaged' offerings that you must have something to interest them.

A key point when you undertake these last two steps is to avoid the temptation to 'come clean' and confess that things are tight. Do that and you put your most valuable assets in a situation where they may feel pressured to come up with something that they can do for you — particularly if you've traditionally had good personal relationships with the account contacts. Also, the thought that you might be under any real pressure can grow into the concern that you may not be around to service or implement any project or product that they might buy from you. Be upbeat and treat this as an account-development meeting — seeking more ways in which you can help these valuable clients to meet their objectives, thereby helping you to meet yours.

3. Revisit All Recent Leads

In good times, there is always some easy money to be made, and, therefore, prospects who express an interest in what we do and then either don't fall in with our timescales, or don't return our calls quickly enough are sometimes allowed to fall by the wayside. Review all of your recent leads (last several months — or whatever timescale makes sense in the context of your sales cycle). Filter out those that came to nothing — but where, for whatever reason, you never got to a 'No!' or to a formal decision on your part to qualify out. If these folks contacted you looking for information, or attended a seminar, or requested a brochure, then at that point in time they had a qualified interest. Re-animate these leads and chase them to ground, once and for all. You'll find in at least some of them that they never got around to making their purchase because they were just too busy and — there was no salesperson driving their decision-making process. Be that salesperson.

4. Seek Referrals

This is classic, basic sales advice — but it is never more important than when times are tough. In every encounter

with active clients or hibernating accounts, and with anyone else you happen to speak with over these coming
months, get into the habit of asking for referrals. During the
good times, the basics get left behind. Look in existing
accounts for referrals to other contacts within that account,
or for referrals to their suppliers and peer organisations.
Speak with everyone you know in business and ask them to
think of anyone to whom you should be speaking. It will get
results. Simple, but effective.

5. Cast Your Net Wider

When things are good, the advice is simple: refine your target
audience. That means knowing your customer base and marketing to them to the exclusion of all others. It also means
being fussy — going only for the high-ticket, high-margin
deals that you deserve. When the going gets tough, it's time to get a little less fussy: go for some of those smaller sales/projects that you would have sniffed at in better times. Be prepared to come down from the mountain.

> Tough times demand flexibility — be prepared to come down from the mountain to consider business you might previously have ignored.

Take that horrified look off your face — we're not suggesting that you compromise your values or your standard of service, simply that you recognise the reality that tighter times demand a more flexible approach to deciding upon who merits

your attention. Nor are we suggesting that you throw all discretion out the window, and market to all comers. There's no need for such drastic action — you'll find that lowering your sights even a little will substantially broaden the target base with which you have to work.

Be careful, however. What you sell to one class of prospects may not appeal to another, perhaps smaller, purchaser. Look carefully at your offerings, and at the new additions to your target base, and repackage what you do to appeal specifically to them. Is there a way to 'modularise' what you do, breaking it down into smaller individually priced elements that smaller clients can use on an as-needed basis? Can you provide financial payment terms that make it easier for the client with shallower pockets to work with you? What can you do to broaden your appeal?

Recognise that you may have to create a brand new range of product/service offerings and marketing approaches to allow you to hit your now wider target base.

6. DON'T Reduce (or increase) Costs

...but DO increase value. The moment you start the 'bargain basement' approach, your existing clients, and all around them, will imagine that they smell 'blood in the water', and this may shake their confidence — driving them further away than ever from doing business with you. No prospect or client ever ran away from more 'bang for his or her buck', however. Look at how you can deliver more — better service, higher quality, better payment terms, whatever — for the same money. Do this by looking at what your targets value and what your competitors deliver. You'll find that you can very often up your value proposition by 100 per cent and still elevate your true cost of sale by only a fraction of that percentage. And — need we say it? — don't even consider pumping up your prices in tough times.

7. Invest More Time and Money

...in marketing and promotion. You've heard it all before: sales is a numbers game. These numbers — particularly the key ratio — are completely different when things tighten. If you were working a 100–10–1 model previously (100 suspects producing 10 prospects, which in turn produced 1 sale), then you know that you're going to have to ramp the input to this funnel to a much higher level to compensate for the slowdown. Do you have to double it? Treble it? Whatever the multiplier, you'll find that you need to have your prospecting machine running continually, in parallel with all other activities, seven days a week. Look at what you can realistically aim to sell to your (new?) target base and set about designing as many ongoing prospecting activities as possible. Ramp up your PR, run value-added seminars and road shows, engage in coordinated mail and fax outs — do whatever you have to do to get your message, and ultimately your sales team, in front of as many prospective clients as possible. If you haven't already done so, consider dedicating some of your team to prospecting alone. Now is not the time to stint on the promotional budget — now more than ever you have to invest in chasing prospects out into the open.

8. Build Lifetime Clients

In general, the easiest and most profitable business to win has always been that won from existing satisfied clients.

Delivering excellent customer service is absolutely essential when there's less business to go around. If you are a direct part of the sales organisation or effort in your company, you are one of those with ultimate responsibility for development of profitable client relationships, and with client retention. No longer can you pass the buck for implementation or delivery to someone else in the organisation — to ensure your future sales, you must take complete ownership and responsibility for the success (as perceived by your client) of all of your sales. This means taking a perhaps unprecedented interest in the successful and quality implementation or delivery of every project, product or service you deliver to your clients. It means ensuring that everyone involved in delivering what you sell understands that you expect them to 'go the extra mile' to satisfy your clients spectacularly. Ensure that all of your sales result in delivering the success and benefit that the client set out to achieve — that way, you start making headway on tomorrow's sales today.

9. Ask the Troops What They Think

Before you charge into putting all of these suggestions into action, see if your team has any more to add to the action plan. Call for input from every department in your company on what its people think you could do to up revenues and drive sales. Don't confine this to your sales and marketing people — frequently your technical and administration people have a keener awareness of what your clients would really like, or would be willing to pay that little extra for. Besides drumming up new ideas, this process will make everyone feel an important part of the organisation's positive drive for increased success — people will much more effectively implement actions that they feel they helped to formulate than ones that they feel have been imposed upon them.

10. Keep Your Chin Up

Hey! I'm not Pollyanna, I'm not a positive-thinking-in-the-face-of-ridiculous-odds nut-ball, but I can assure you that unless you stay optimistic, you're dead. Don't feel that you or your business is unique in its suffering, and that all is lost — it's that kind of thinking that fuels dips in consumer confidence. Whatever you're facing, you'll find that others have come through worse, and that things always get better — and this happens all the faster for those who keep their heads and remain focused and optimistic.

Too many people fold up their tents and head for home at the first sign of bad weather. Don't be one of them. Businesses can survive, and even thrive, if they keep their heads and do what needs to be done to cope with more challenging times. Decide what you need to do to ride the storm out, and then focus all of your energies upon doing it.

The sky is never really falling, unless we collectively wish it down upon ourselves.

Strategy 32

The New Art of
Hiring Smart

The New Art of Hiring Smart

Good People Grow Business

It's the best of times and the worst of times too — if people problems are coming between you and the commercial success that you see your peers enjoying.

If you're either experiencing excessive staff turnover or finding that the people you're hiring simply 'don't fit in', use the following six steps, *The New Art of Hiring Smart*, to ensure that you get more of the people you need.

Step 1. Determine the True Cost of Turnover

The Saratoga Institute (www.saratogainstitute.com) publishes a simple formula for calculating turnover cost. Take the annual salary for any job where you have excessive turnover, add a typical 30 per cent for benefits, and calculate 25 per cent of the total. That's the *absolute minimum* it costs you every time that position turns over — if you provide any other benefits, or incur any other costs, it's actually much, much more. Multiply this figure by the number of times the position turns over. Do this for every job where you have turnover. Scary, huh? Add other costs, like share of overhead, recruitment costs (agency fees, advertising, travel, etc), training costs, lost production/opportunity cost while the position is empty, and morale costs. Now that I have your attention, let's do something about the problem.

Step 2. Identify Hiring Problems and Mistakes

Identify any part of your organisation with 'people problems', and find out what's causing them by:

- Asking your department and human resource managers why, in their opinion, these departments have turnover, why people quit, get fired, or become problematic;

- Conducting exit interviews — ask each person who leaves the company what could you have done to help them succeed and to prevent them from leaving. Don't be fooled by 'pay more money';

- Asking your top people what they like about their jobs and how you can make their jobs better — try to replicate whatever they like throughout the organisation;

- Looking at the people doing the hiring, and asking them (or asking yourself): Do they need training? Do they have a system that works? Do they take hiring new people seriously?

Step 3. Recruit People who FIT Your Jobs

To do this, you must:
- *Understand the Job and Develop a Competency-Based Job Description*

  It is critical that you document what competencies all of your jobs require from a technical, educational,

215

experience, and industrial know-how basis — otherwise, how can you know what you're looking for?

- *Match People to Jobs*

Harvard Business Review conducted a huge study of 360,000 people, in fourteen industries, over a twenty-year period, in an attempt to identify what made for job success. They found that, regardless of any other factor, people are successful only when they are matched to their jobs. They must have the right level of *Learning Abilities*; have a motivational *Interest* in the work; and their *Behavioural Make-up* or personality must equip them to do the job well.

You cannot get the information necessary to match people to jobs from candidates' CVs, or from conventional interviews. The only way you can uncover this information is by formal assessment of candidates using assessments designed specially for the task.

Profiles International's *The Profile* was designed specifically for this task — you can find more information on it at: www.profilesinternational.com/products/profileXT.asp

Step 4. Prospect Innovatively for Candidates

Consider additional sources that you may not be using, such as:

- *Employee Bonus for Referrals of Candidates You Employ*

- *Physically or Mentally Disadvantaged*

- *Senior Citizens*
  The retired community is a rich source of motivated candidates for many empty positions.

- *Companies that have Announced Cutbacks*
  Contact the personnel and department managers in organisations announcing cutbacks, and describe the candidate you are seeking.

- *Set up Educational Relationships*
  Find the universities, colleges, or schools that support your industry through their curriculum, and develop relationships with them.

Step 5. Prepare for and Conduct a Winning Interview

Preparing for an interview is just as important as the interview itself.

- *Review the Job Description*
  In advance of the interview, clarify in your mind the job requirements, and the kind of competencies you expect to find in the person you're looking for.

217

- *Develop Lead Questions*

  Lead questions are questions based on the job description — designed to bring out answers that will lead to follow-up questions.

The interview itself has three parts:

- *The Open*

  No candidate likes doing interviews — they are viewed simply as a necessary evil. The *Open* has two objectives: first, to put the applicant at ease and build rapport. The better the rapport you create, the better the information you receive. Second, you want to set the agenda and timetable. Explain the sequence for the interview and approximately how long you will be together for.

  Your overall objectives for the *Open* are to create excitement about the job and to put your candidate at ease.

- *The Body*

  This section of the interview is where you use your lead questions. When doing so, think:

  - *Can this person do the job?*

    Have they the necessary qualifications, experience, and competencies that you know are necessary for success in the position? Do their *Learning Abilities* match those demanded by the job?

  - *Will this person do the job?*

    If you've satisfied yourself that the candidate has what it takes to do the job successfully, your next task is to ensure that they are motivated to be successful in the position. Is the nature of the work sufficiently motivating for them to ensure success? This can usually be determined only through assessment of the candidate's *Motivational Interests* using assessments like *The Profile* (mentioned above). The purpose of the interview in this regard is then to probe any areas of concern uncovered by the assessment process.

◆ *Will this person fit our corporate culture?*
Being capable and motivated to do the job well is sufficient only if you are sure that the candidate will also be a good fit to your company in terms of its culture, existing team-members, clients, processes, and so on. Again, the extent of this match is best determined using a pre-interview assessment like *The Profile*, with the interview providing an opportunity to probe any areas where the candidate seems to be a poor match to the position.

Listen carefully and take notes. Later, review your notes carefully and form your opinions.

● *The Close*
The Close is no less important than the two previous stages of the interview, allowing for both sides to summarise and agree next steps.

In a book that I highly recommend — *Hire with Your Head* by Lou Adler — there's a suggested closing statement

Hire with Your Head, by Lou Adler, is an excellent source of information on these key topics.

that can be used with all candidates, especially those who will make the next cut:

> *'Although we're seeing other fine candidates, I person-ally think that you have a very fine background. We'll get back to you in a few days, but what are your thoughts about this new position?'*

This close creates a sense of competition and job attractiveness; expresses sincere interest in the candidate; and allows the interviewer to gauge how much interest the candidate has in the position.

Step Six: Continually Refine Your Practices

Books like Lou Adler's *Hire with Your Head*, and seminars and workshops on best-practice hiring, run by organisations like Profiles International, will help you continually to refine your skills in this key area. Your local Profiles office can let you know what events are scheduled in your area (find your local representative by e-mailing:

Profiles@ProfilesInternational.com)

People are your most important asset — shouldn't you invest at least as much effort in attracting, recruiting and retaining them as you invest in winning and retaining customers?

Strategy 33

What Goes Around

What Goes Around

See Your Managers' Strengths
from Every Angle

A senior manager announces his decision to move to a competitor and the senior management team convenes a crisis-management meeting to figure how the organisation will ever survive without this key individual. Meanwhile, however, for the rest of the team, it's party time! The champagne is out, everyone's wearing funny hats, blowing noise-makers, and toasting their good fortune. The conversation topic *du jour* is '*With that clown gone, maybe now we can get on with business.*'

What happened? How can someone so valued by senior management work so badly with the troops on the ground? The reality is that most senior managers have no awareness whatever of how they or their fellow managers are perceived throughout their organisations — at a time when so much is spoken about achievement of corporate goals through team-based efforts. It's no wonder that recent research by Profiles International revealed that over 30 per cent of all people changing jobs are doing so to get away from their bosses. They're not leaving their jobs — they're leaving their managers!

This sort of disaster can happen only in an environment where the performance of management is appraised using traditional 'boss-down' appraisals, with performance of managers assessed only by their direct bosses.

This traditional approach means that the views of those who most directly experience the effectiveness (or otherwise) of a manager's performance — peers and direct reports — are never tapped. If your success depends to any extent upon your team, that's just not acceptable any more.

Multi-Rater Feedback

Modern business has rendered the traditional 'boss-down' appraisal extinct, and a more appropriate approach to assessing management competencies and performance has emerged. That new approach is *Multi-Rater Feedback*, and Profiles *Checkpoint* is an excellent example of this new model.

CHECKPOINT MULTI-RATER FEEDBACK

Every year, more than 250,000 managers worldwide go through this new annual appraisal process, using the Profiles *Checkpoint Multi-Rater Feedback System* — a system that provides managers and leaders with an opportunity to receive an evaluation of their job performance from the people around them — their *Boss*, their *Peers* (fellow managers), and their *Direct Reports* (the people whose work they supervise). From this feedback, managers can compare the opinions of others with their own perceptions, positively identify their strengths, and pinpoint the areas of their job performance that could be improved.

The *Checkpoint* process is concerned with a manager's job performance in eight universal leadership and management competencies, and eighteen skill sets:

Communication
- Listens to others
- Processes information
- Communicates effectively

Leadership
- Instils trust
- Provides direction
- Delegates responsibility

Adaptability
- Adjusts to circumstances
- Thinks creatively

Relationships
- Builds personal relationships
- Facilitates team success

Task Management
- Works efficiently
- Works competently

Production
- Takes action
- Achieves results

Development of Others
- Cultivates individual talents
- Motivates successfully

Personal Development
- Displays commitment
- Seeks improvement

How Does it Work?

Each participant completes an evaluation — a process that takes about 15 minutes. They are guaranteed anonymity (except for the 'Boss') and urged to be honest and objective in their responses. Participants complete their feedback via the Internet, or on paper if desired, and results from all participants are compiled in a report that is returned to the manager.

Checkpoint reports have colourful graphs and charts, as well as narrative descriptions of the results, to help the manager to read, understand, and effectively use the data for self-development. The report has a special personal-growth section that coaches the manager and helps improve performance in development areas.

Modern business has rendered the traditional top-down appraisal extinct.

The *Checkpoint* report also encourages managers to link directly into an online system called *Checkpoint SkillBuilder* which takes them through the step-by-step process of developing a comprehensive and personalised development plan. You can read more about the Checkpoint system on the Web at: www.profilesinternational.com

Round and Round...

The upshot is a more detailed and objective assessment of a manager's strengths, and of any areas where additional development might be required. This assessment then forms the basis of a development plan agreed between

225

managers and their bosses — which ensures that not only are the managers in question fully aware of the dynamics of their relationships with the people around them, but that they are also effectively locked into the organisation by the commitment of the organisation to their on-going skill development.

After a period of six or twelve months, the process is run again; the effectiveness of the development plan is assessed; and new development goals are set for the following period. This is key. *Multi-Rater Feedback* produces its most impressive results when employed in a closed loop of:

> *Feedback…review and produce individual development plan…execute…development…plan…review…feedback…*

…and so on. Repeating the exercise regularly ensures that managers can keep their fingers on the many important pulses in their fast-changing organisations.

Multi-Rater Feedback v. 'Boss-Down' Appraisals

There are several reasons why managers at all levels are eagerly embracing this approach to performance appraisal.

Equitable

For the manager being appraised, *Multi-Rater* appraisals differ from boss-down appraisals in the same way that Judge and Jury courts differ from 'Hanging Judge' courts. Managers benefit from a wide variety of feedback upon their actual job performance, and, to be deemed top-performing managers, are no longer solely dependent upon the extent to which they have developed a good rapport with their direct boss.

Proven Effectiveness

For the appraising 'Boss', there is the confidence that positive change is more likely when an appraisal draws upon multiple sources trusted by the manager. *Multi-Rater* appraisals have been shown to be more effective than boss-down appraisals in driving a manager to make necessary behavioural changes or to improve

> *The cycle is key:*
> *Feedback...*
> *Review...*
> *Plan & Develop...*
> *Review...*
> *Feedback...*
> *and so on.*

management skills. If your boss says that you need some improvement in some particular area, you may think '*What would she know?!*' or explain it away as a '*personality thing*'. If, however, eleven different people of your choosing — people with whom you work closely and whose views you trust and value — send you the same message, you really have to listen.

Team Motivation

Multi-Rater Feedback systems also have a positive team-building effect. Research has proven the motivating value of the exercise for those involved as reviewers — who are sent a clear message that their opinions are valued, and that they can help effect some positive change in the management where required.

Traditional reviews have given way to this much more effective tool for management development, with their use increasingly mandated in Fortune 500 organisations.

Used regularly as an integral part of a strategic development plan, 360-degree appraisals can lead to more consistent management development, better alignment of corporate goals with personal-development objectives, more open communication, and better team balance.

Strategy 34

Day Before Vacation

Day Before Vacation

Prioritise and Commit for Success

Have you recently felt that there aren't enough hours in the day to get everything done — that life is just whizzing past you?

If so, don't despair — it simply means that tough times have knocked you just a little out of focus.

To get back on top of things, you'll need to revisit a time when you were in total control, and at a recent Zig Ziglar seminar we learned how to do just that!

Bring that Day-Before-Vacation commitment to bear — every day!

Think about your last day in work before you went on your most recent holiday. Didn't you get as much done in that day as you'd normally get done in two, three, or even four days? (Be honest!) Let's look at that day before vacation and see what you did.

On the night preceding the day before your holidays, you probably sat down with a piece of paper and listed all of the things that had to get finished the following day — your *gotta*s ('I gotta do this, and I gotta...'). Then you committed that they'd all be done by the time you left the office next day. Right?

On the morning of the day before your vacation, you arrived at the office on time — maybe even early. But you didn't head for the coffee machine — no, you got straight into the first gotta on your list. You likely also did things in a slightly different order from usual — I'll bet you took the least favoured, most distasteful task on your list and got it out of the way quickly, instead of having it hanging overhead all day long (the way you normally would!) Once that *dog* was shot, you were feeling pretty good, and so you tore into the next task on your list, and the next one after that. If anyone came to chat about last night's match, you politely but firmly informed them that you were just too busy — and got back to business.

As you completed each of your *gotta*s, you found that your energy level rose, so that by halfway through the day you were really 'buzzing' with a sense of accomplishment that drove your enthusiasm level ever higher, raising your mood and painting a smile on your face. Your obviously energised and enthusiastic demeanour infected your colleagues — they started to ramp up the effort, to smile a little more, and they became similarly enthusiastic. The atmosphere in the office got a little extra spark, and this lifted you even further.

At the end of the day, you had all of your *gotta*s completed. You were as high as if you'd been on high-octane caffeine — even if you hadn't had a drop all day! In fact, you felt so

231

energised that, with your desk cleared of a lot of stuff that had been hanging around for a while, you were then actually looking forward to getting back to the very place that had created such a pressing need for a restful holiday, right? You felt good. Now, that's focus!

So, what did you do that day to get so focused? Let's have a look.

First, You Created a *Vision*

('By the time I leave tomorrow, I'll have cleared my desk and put my affairs in such good order that I can be spared for the next two weeks.')

When your vision gets knocked offline by events around you, you are like a €10 billion guided missile without a target — you can fly around in circles looking pretty impressive, but eventually you're going to run out of fuel and crash and burn. If your vision has been hammered by recent economic changes, get working on a new one — now! Take some time to figure out what you really want for yourself, your family and your business. Get it clear in your head and paint this target in front of you every day.

Second, You Formulated a Set of Goals that would Deliver Your Vision — Your *Gottas*

('I gotta call Deiric, I gotta....')

Having a great vision is no good unless you formulate clear, achievable goals that ensure your vision comes to pass. You must plot a course that will take you from where you are now to your target, with checkpoints that let you know when you go off course.

Third, You Made a Commitment

('I absolutely must get these tasks completed by the time I leave the office tomorrow.')

This is the most common stumbling block that people tend to hit, even if they are accustomed to planning by creating compelling visions and formulating achievable goals. They fail to commit. If you've ever made a New Year's resolution that you failed to complete, you know what happens to plans without commitment. If there's no commitment, the fault is most likely with your vision — it simply isn't compelling enough; otherwise, the commitment would follow normally. If you were fatally ill and had just one month to live, but could get a cure if you had one million more Euros than your current total net worth, would you get the money? Of course you would — or you'd kill yourself trying even before the month was out! You know that your vision is right when it has the same sense of compelling urgency. A real commitment gets you immediately off the ground and in search of your target.

> *A real commitment gets you immediately off the ground in search of your target.*

So, before you spend one more day out of focus in your life, stop and look at your life carefully. Be sure that your guidance mechanism has a clear target encoded into it, and that you've mapped a route to target that makes you want to take off right now! Get that Day-Before-Vacation feeling every day!

'We must use
time as a tool,
not as a crutch.'
JOHN F. KENNEDY

Strategy 35

Killer Sales Campaigns

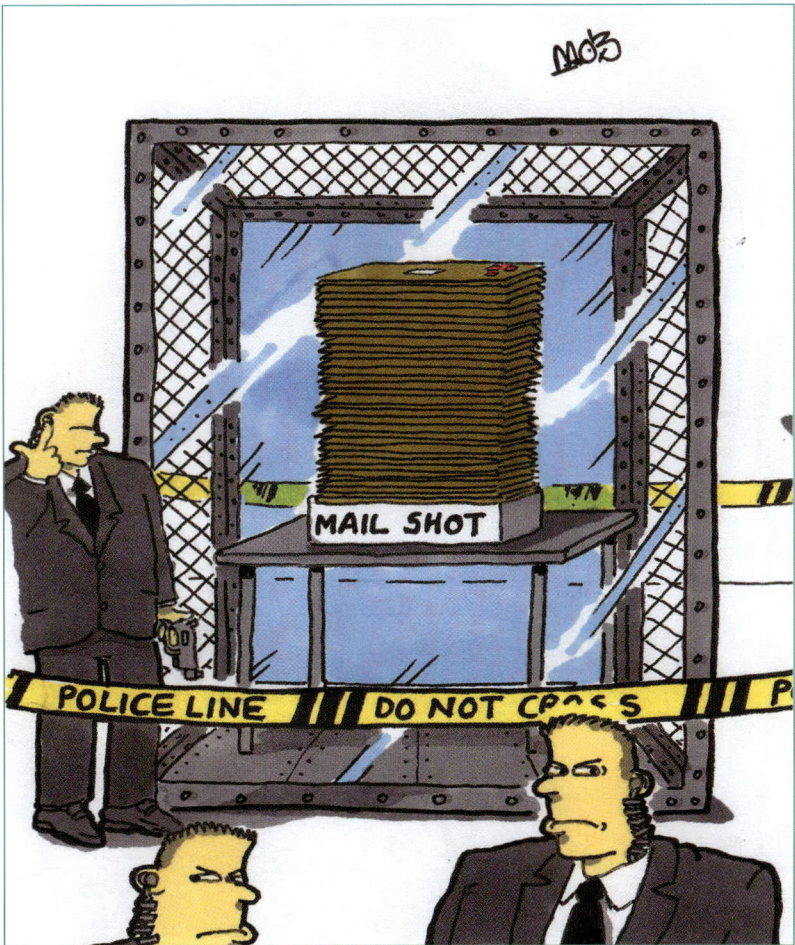

Killer Sales Campaigns

How is Your Sales Heart Beating?

Sales are the beating heart at the centre of every successful organisation, and successful sales campaigns keep that heart beating.

The success or failure or your campaign is decided long before you decide what initiatives you're going to pursue. It is decided when you set your goals for the campaign. Clear goals make successful campaigns. The following simple steps will help you to create killer sales campaigns every time.

First, Ask Yourself: 'How will I know when my campaign has been successful?'

The first thing to decide is precisely what objective the campaign must achieve. Typical objectives might revolve around selling a particular number of units, achieving a given revenue target, building a specific prospect pipeline, etc. Clearly define the objective of the campaign in terms like, 'We'll know the campaign is successful when…'

- '…we have sold 200 units of X product'

- '…we have added fifty new customers to our customer base'

- '…we have achieved revenues of X, with a margin of Y'.

You may have multiple objectives for a given campaign — be sure that they are all SMART — **S**pecific, **M**easurable, **A**chievable, **R**ealistic, and **T**imed.

Then, Ask Yourself: 'What do I have to do to achieve this?'

Let's say that your campaign objective was the first one outlined above — 'to sell 200 units of X product'. Follow these six steps to determine what actions your campaign will need to include to ensure success.

1. Look at Your Typical Sale — How Many Units of Product Does.it Entail?

Let's say your typical sale is 10 units to a customer. Divide this figure into your end target — this will tell you how many customers you have to sell to, to achieve your target. In the example, you'll need to close twenty new customers.

2. Look at Your 'Close Rate'

Your close rate is the percentage of qualified prospects that ultimately become customers. If you don't have accurate figures from your records, estimate your close rate on the basis of your experience. Always estimate conservatively. For example, in my business, seven years of research show that we achieve a 2-in-5 close rate (40 per cent) with well-qualified prospects. Applying that close rate to the example tells you that to land twenty new clients, you'd need to present to fifty well-qualified prospects. By the way, 'well-qualified' means that they need your product, can afford your product, and are prepared to meet with you to discuss what benefits it might bring to them.

3. Look at Your 'Qualification Rate'

Now look at how many initial contacts or 'touches' with suspects (suspected prospects) you will need to have in order to provide you with these fifty well-qualified prospects. In my business, we use mail-shot, fax-shot and seminar activity to reach out to suspects. We achieve a 1-in-10 hit rate in identifying prospects who potentially need the service that we provide, and are prepared to meet with us to discuss their requirements — these are our 'well-qualified' prospects. Applying this to the example means that you're going to need to 'touch' five hundred suspects over the course of the campaign to achieve your campaign objective.

4. Convert this Information into an Overview of the Activity Your Campaign Should Be Driving

Let's assume that this campaign will run over a ten-month period. You now know that your campaign must generate:

- Five hundred suspect 'touches' overall, which is an average of fifty per month, or approximately thirteen per week;

- Fifty prospect presentations overall, which is an average of five per month, or approximately two per week;

- Twenty new customers overall, which is an average of two per month, or approximately one every two weeks.

5. Decide What Initiatives Will Deliver These Results to You

Now you have an idea of what you'll have to do to achieve your objectives and sub-objectives. The challenge is to figure out what actions will deliver these results to you. Look at the sort of initiatives that might create the required number of touches, presentations and close opportunities. Typical approaches include:

> *The success or failure of a sales campaign is determined long before you decide precisely what initiatives you'll pursue.*

- Mail- and fax-shots

- Seminars/In-store promotions

- Advertising/PR

- Whatever else has worked for you or your competitors in the past.

This is where you spend whatever budget you have to invest in your campaign. Look at which initiatives will give

239

you the 'best bang for your buck' in terms of hitting the specific numbers of suspects and prospects that you now know you need. If one or other of these initiatives has previously shown itself to be more successful, spread your budget accordingly.

6. Keep an Eye on Progress

If you're sensible, you'll take the attitude that your campaign plan represents your best guess at what will be successful for you, and you'll review its progress with the open-minded attitude that you'll change it should it not prove as successful as you had originally hoped. Review your progress regularly — weekly, if appropriate. Have you hit your 'touch', prospect presentation, and close rates for this week? If not, why not? Do you need to make any course corrections? Do you need to redouble your efforts next week? Is the original campaign strategy still valid? If not, change course immediately. Review progress on a frequent basis and you'll assure your campaign success.

Killer sales campaigns are less about the actual initiatives you undertake, and more about knowing precisely what you're trying to achieve; having a clear means for measuring your progress towards achieving it; reviewing your progress on a regular basis; and having the guts to change direction midstream if progress demands it.

Take this sensible approach and the success is assured — all of your campaigns will be *natural-born killers*.

240

Strategy 36

Put Your Clients on the Map

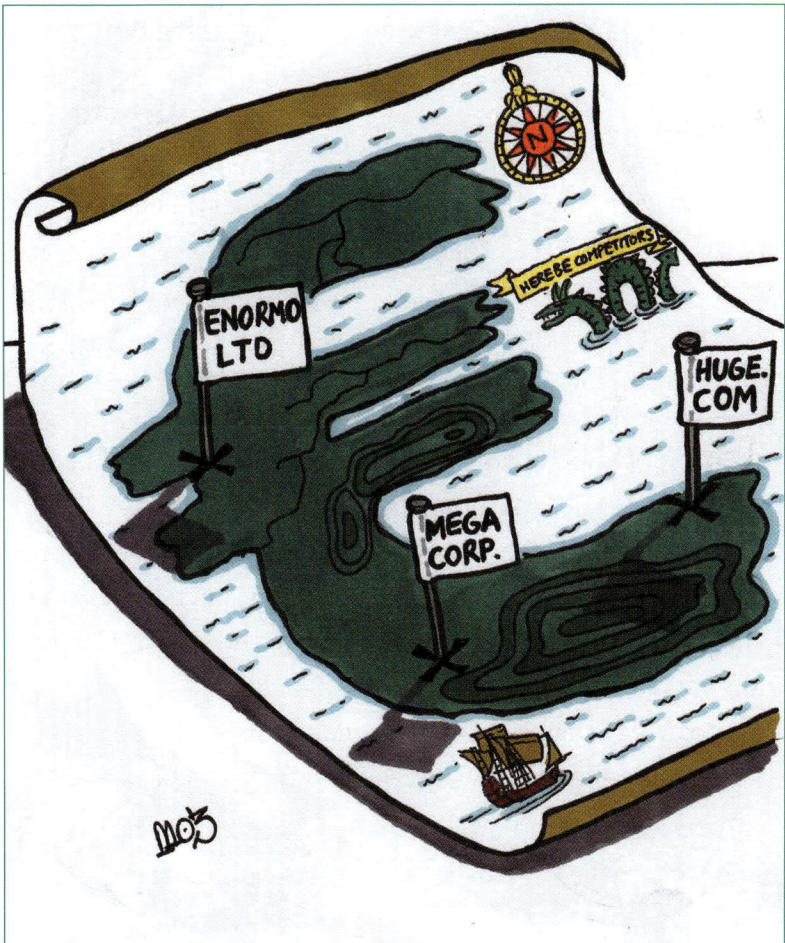

Put Your Clients on the Map

Chart a Course to Large-Account Success

You must put your major customers on the map, or someone else will.

Your world has changed. The emphasis on the acquisition of new customers, at whatever cost — where marketing was undertaken on a grand scale, and we were all just numbers, to be most effectively reached by mass-marketing techniques — is no more. Suddenly, there's the universal realisation that existing customers are faster and easier to sell to, that business is much less expensive to win from existing customers than from strangers. The new order is 'one-on-one' marketing and loyalty building — to ensure retention of those customers who will consistently generate good-margin business. And the only way to retain these valuable customers is by building solid, lasting and mutually beneficial relationships with them. But that's not easy.

Developing relationships takes a lot of time and effort, and is consequently extremely expensive. Limited resources mean that you have to be sure that the clients you choose to develop are worth the effort — that they will give you a good return over time. Trying to be all things to all customers just won't work — spread yourself too thinly and you're setting yourself up for a fall. The investment is such that you simply can't afford to fail — you're almost betting the shop.

The key to success in your selected large accounts is understanding the power dynamics of the target organisation: who makes the decisions; who assists; and who holds the power? This implies that the team selling to such key accounts has a solid handle on the structure of the decision-making group in the account, is clear on how each member of that group views the selling organisation, and has a uniform plan to apply the resources at their disposal systematically to the effective development of relations with each member of the decision-making group.

The only way to retain valuable customers is to build solid, lasting and mutually beneficial relationships.

To be effective, an account team must face a number of significant challenges.

1. Identify all Members of the Decision-making Group

   ...there's no point in selling hard to one or more members of the group if an unknown member can exercise a veto and kill you in the account.

2. Rank Them in Order of Influence/Importance

   ...knowing who really makes the decisions, and who plays what role in the decision-making process is crucial.

243

3. Identify What Motivates Them

...mass marketing insists that we all think the same, that we will all share a common view of the world. One-on-one marketing recognises that everyone has their individual turn-ons, and that each individual must be sold to according to their particular motivations. There's no point in offering the Chief Financial Officer the most comfortable truck on the market, or offering the driver the least expensive truck on the market — sell to their motivations.

4. Determine How They Feel about You and Your Company

...if a key decision-maker has no time for you or your organisation, work is needed. If, however, they think you're wonderful, then less effort may be required — freeing up resources that can be used elsewhere.

5. Produce a Plan to Develop Each Contact Continually

...knowing what turns them on, and how they feel about your organisation, the team must plan to undertake whatever actions are necessary to improve the relationship.

6. Communicating This Plan to Ensure a Consistent Focused Team Effort

...if all team-members are not pulling together towards a common set of relationship-development objectives, the effort will be less successful — and the only way that they can pull together effectively is if the view of the account is developed by the team as a whole.

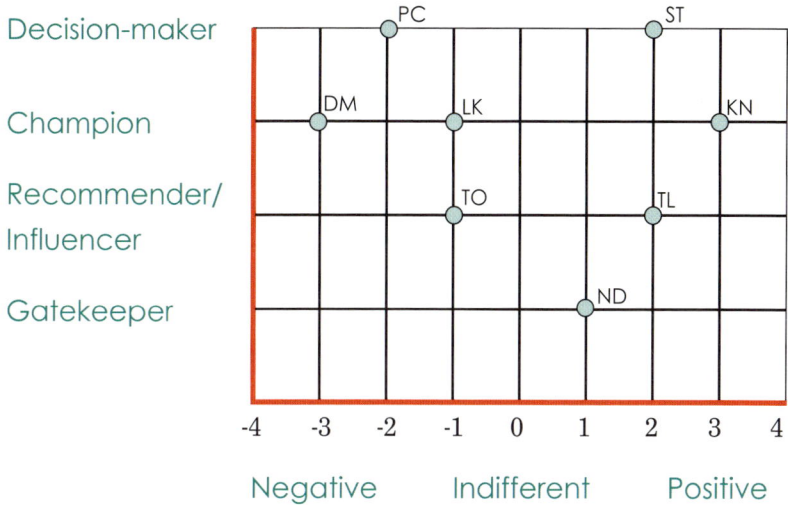

			PC			ST	
Decision-maker

Champion

Recommender/
Influencer

Gatekeeper

-4 -3 -2 -1 0 1 2 3 4

Negative   Indifferent   Positive

Mapping Your Accounts

Use a Relationship Map like that shown above to make this easier. Across the bottom is a gauge of how the various contacts in the account feel about your organisation and its offerings — *Negative* through *Indifferent* to *Positive*. Up the side is a range of useful classifications for the range of players found in most decision-making groups:

- A **Decision-maker** is the person who can give you a 'yes'. Anyone having the power of veto would also fall under this heading. There is often more than one individual who may exercise this power.

- A **Champion** is generally a **Decision-maker** or **Recommender/Influencer** who has chosen to drive a project or offering within their organisation.

- **Recommenders/Influencers** are any other persons who have an input in the decision, but have no absolute

245

yes or *no* power. Examples might include end-users — the person who must ultimately use the PC or drive the purchased truck.

- The **Gatekeeper** defines who is allowed to play the game. Typically, this person is a purchasing manager or the head of the department who will be most affected by the planned purchase (for example, the IT Manager if the acquisition is a computer). It could also be a politically strong administration person like the CEO's secretary.

> *Put all key account contacts on your map and rate them* Negative, Positive *or* Indifferent.

All members of the decision-making group can be placed somewhere on this map by assigning them a rank and a *Negative/Positive* rating. Once the team has agreed on where each decision-maker goes on the map (and it is imperative that mapping is on the basis of a team view), it becomes apparent to all where the selling organisation stands in the accounts, and who must be developed in order to improve that standing. The team-members should strive to ensure that they have the entire decision group mapped, and that all are as far to the right on the map as possible. Again, resources may dictate that not all group-members can be developed equally, so decisions can be made on the relative investment required to improve the overall *Positive* index of the map.

Mapped contacts are moved rightwards by development of a plan for each contact. This plan should:

- Recognise that particular contact's personal turn-ons;

- Include a number of specific 'to-dos' — actions designed to improve the relationship with that contact. These actions should be practical, measurable, and should have 'complete by' dates;

- Outline what information is required in order to improve the standing with that individual, and identify which team-member(s) is/are best placed to get hold of that information. The plan should also ensure that all of those having any day-to-day contact with the account understand what information is required — this should be to the front of the minds of sales and support people making calls on decision-makers;

> *Focus your efforts on those initiatives that drive key account contacts as far right on your map as possible.*

- Be reviewed by the team on a regular basis, with the map being updated on the basis of team input — and progress being measured by comparison with previous maps.

Map your major customers, and watch them put you, and your efforts, on the map.

'You can close more business in two months by becoming interested in other people than you can in two years by trying to get people interested in you.'

DALE CARNEGIE

248

Strategy 37

Carrot, Stick or What?

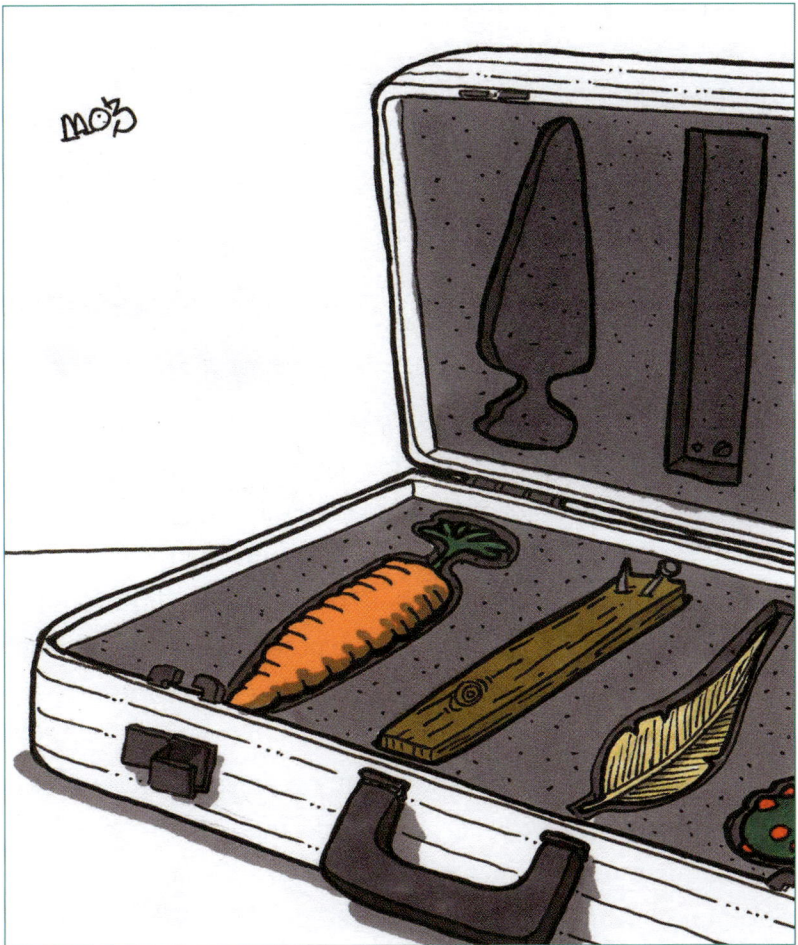

Carrot, Stick or What?

To Push or to Pull —
That is the Question!

How would you like to have all of your team chomping at the bit to do what you need them to do to make your business successful?

Everyone wants that elusive ingredient — motivation — in the people to whom they entrust the development of their businesses. Well, sorry to turn the lights to dim so quickly, but here's the bad news: YOU CANNOT MOTIVATE ANYONE TO DO ANYTHING — people do what they do because they want to, not because you want them to. And they'll only want to do what you want them to do when the outcome of doing so appeals to them in some way. It is all in their hands, not yours. So, for practical business purposes, motivation is *getting people to do what you want them to do, because* THEY *want to do it*.

We are all motivated to action by two types of motivators — *intrinsic* and *extrinsic*. *Extrinsic* motivation happens when some outside factor causes us to take action — for example, '*Work an extra six hours and I'll pay you double*

250

time'. Most management 'motivation' is purely extrinsic, and amounts to little more than manipulation — enlisting promises, bribes and flattery to get things done.

The problem with extrinsic motivation is that it rarely has any useful long-term effect. Use extrinsic motivators to energise your team and you'll find yourself trapped in a cycle where those 'motivators' must get bigger and better all of the time just to repeat the same results. How long does the motivational effect of a salary increase last? Often only as long as it takes to see the post-tax figure! Traditional extrinsic approaches to motivation are all but useless aids to boosting long-term employee morale and productivity, or to stemming employee turnover.

> *Motivation is getting people to do what you need them to do — because they want to.*

So, what about *intrinsic* motivation? This happens when you take action for internal reasons — for example, when you work an extra six hours because you feel that the project you're working on is one so worthwhile that you want to see it completed. Everything we do is ultimately determined by the values we hold. Values are what we truly care about — the qualities and standards we hold dear and aspire to. These values determine our attitudes and behaviours, and determine what will motivate us to action. When people take action because the likely outcome of that action appeals directly to what they value, you have true motivation — and time spent developing that *is* an investment

251

with long-term returns. That's why the most successful leaders and motivators are those who (wittingly or un-wittingly) uncover their followers' intrinsic motivations, and take time to match these with the extrinsic motivators they have at their disposal.

Easy? Not at all. People are motivated by unmet needs and, unfortunately, these will vary from person to person according to their particular circumstances, values and beliefs, education, family background, personality, and work experience. The only way to figure out what is important to your people is to ask them, and then to listen carefully. Ask often enough, and show your willingness to take action upon whatever you uncover, and your people will begin to let you know what is important to them — allowing you to figure out how to package those extrinsic 'motivators' you have at

your disposal in a manner that will meet their particular needs. This dialogue can be fostered with mechanisms as simple as frequent one-to-one discussions or well-considered surveys. There are no quick fixes, and this is not a one-off exercise; to be successful this has to become an integral part of the way you do business.

While working upon uncovering what your particular people need to be motivated, be aware that a lot of recent research has shown that what motivated people even as recently as ten years ago is no longer necessarily relevant today. For example, modern employees view it as a right to have market-level remuneration in return for their efforts — so compensation is no longer a true motivator. In addition to a good salary and benefits package, you MUST now also provide:

> *Everyone now routinely expects market-level remuneration — so money's no longer much of a motivator.*

- Development Opportunities — if you don't develop your people at the pace they desire, they'll find someone who can. People want to grow.

- Balance — new research shows that the modern worker's priorities are: leisure, family and work — in that order. Make number three the priority at the expense of one and two and you may well strongly motivate them — to move elsewhere.

- Input to Decisions — modern employees feel strongly that they deserve input into any decisions that might affect them. Ignore this *right* at your peril.

- Communication with Management — modern employees are educated and confident and demand ongoing communication with their management.

- Worthwhile Goals — to hold their attention, people need the buzz of worthwhile short-term goals, and lots of feedback on their success (or failure) in achieving these goals.

- Interesting Work — much of the research on employee satisfaction over the past five years has emphasised the important role that interesting, challenging work plays in motivating people.

Take these three seemingly straightforward steps to build a highly motivated team:

1. Right now: Honestly review the checklist above and, if anything on it is not a feature of the way you interface with your team, figure out how you can make it so in the shortest time possible.

2. ASAP: Establish a programme to ensure that you establish a frequently updated profile of just what motivates each and every member of your team, and use this information to match the extrinsic motivators you have at your disposal to best meet their requirements.

3. Ongoing Basis: Look carefully at the extrinsic motivators you have at your disposal and use your knowledge of your people's values and needs to match them to their intrinsic needs.

This will energise your team and assure your success. Now, is that a carrot, or what?

Strategy 38

The Final Hurdle

The Final Hurdle

Don't Fall at the Last Fence

You're on the home straight: your prospect has bought into what you're offering, and there's only one last hurdle — the final negotiation. Ask any seasoned campaigner, and they'll tell you that this is where all too many great deals suddenly die. What's the secret of sailing safely over that last hurdle?

The secret is that there is no secret — just a set of common-sense rules to observe, and some preparations to undertake.

Final negotiations are no different from any other part of the sales cycle in that success depends largely upon careful planning. Understand what you absolutely *must* take away from the table, how much (if any) you're prepared to concede, and be prepared to walk away if you can't reach agreement within these bounds. Similarly, know what you would *ideally* like to achieve, and what you can reasonably expect, given limitations like your client's budget.

Think about your game plan — the order in which you will address the various elements in the upcoming negotiation — and plan a path through the negotiation which will most naturally lead your prospect to accepting your negotiation objectives. For this to be successful, you need to have walked through each and every play, anticipating objections and formulating responses that return you to your planned course and desired outcome.

In the words of a seasoned campaigner: *'If sales is courtship, then negotiation is foreplay — the slower it goes, the better.'* Generally, the only reason for maintaining the fast-forward pace of the sales cycle into the final negotiation is the concern that the deal might slip away if not closed *now*. Relax — if there wasn't a genuine interest in doing business, you'd hardly be in a final negotiation, right? Slow it down.

> *Relax into negotiation — if they weren't interested, would you even be talking?*

Some purchasers like to introduce a little drama into a final negotiation by raising points not previously on the table. You can do a lot to address this problem before it happens. Be sure to:

- Know their requirements inside out, and understand how badly they need what you're offering;

- Know their budgets and timescales;

- Know the strengths and weaknesses of what you're offering, and how you stack up against your competition;

- Know who really makes the final decision, and who else has any input.

The only way to get this information is to ask for it at every opportunity — up to, and including, the final negotiation

itself. When you've asked, simply shut up and listen. Ambushes are not effective if you see them coming.

When the negotiation swings toward price, ask for confirmation that all other obstacles have been cleared. If you understand what is most important to your client, and have effectively sold other aspects of your offering like delivery timescales, quality, solution, and so forth, you'll have a better feel for how much importance the client places on price per se, and you'll better understand whether or not you have to move on price at all, and, if so, by how much.

When clearing all pre-price obstacles, remember that while you may have a perfect match to your client's requirements, you cannot assume that they recognise this fact. Be sure to stress the value of the *whole* of your offering. Don't assume that some valuable aspect of your offering that has not been identified as key by your client has no value to them. Build a clear vision of the value of your offering in your client's mind before getting into price negotiations.

If you find that you must give a price concession, seek something in return, and offer upfront no more than 75 per cent of any concession you are prepared to make. Then hold firm. If the prospect detects any chink in your resolve, they will continue the pressure for downward negotiations in price. Professional purchasers will return to previously closed aspects of the deal to try to shave off a little more advantage for themselves — only to return to the price issue again later. Waver, and you and your deal will die the slow and painful 'death of a thousand cuts'. Use the little you've held back on when you are certain that it will secure the business for you.

Even when the dealing is effectively finished, negotiations can still drag on unless you make a concerted effort to close. Happily, human nature is such that the value we place on anything is often inversely proportional to its free availability, so use this fact to formulate effective final closing plays:

- 'Prices will go up shortly, but for a commitment now I may be able to fix prices at this level for the lifetime of this deal...'

- 'I'd have to get board approval for this level of discount, but if I could...'

Human nature is such that the value we place upon things is often inversely proportional to their free availability — use this knowledge in your closes.

While it may sound a little like the slick car-salesman close, it is legitimate and it does work.

Final negotiations are never really easy, but if you plan, slow things down, anticipate ambushes, box clever on price, and close on scarcity, you'll sail cleanly over that final hurdle every time.

259

'The hero is no braver than an ordinary man, but he is brave five minutes longer.'
RALPH WALDO EMERSON

Strategy 39

Once Beaten, Twice Smart

Once Beaten, Twice Smart

Turn Today's Losses into Tomorrow's Wins

Achieving a consistent 70 per cent hit rate with the sales you pursue would probably keep you quite happy. Yet a 70 per cent hit rate means losing almost half as many sales as you win. Most would accept that these losses are the price paid for the wins they value so much, and write them off. But what about the investment of time and effort in those lost sales? The challenge is to turn short-term failures into longer-term successes, to get some return on the investment of time, effort and resources.

If you can achieve this, losses become part of winning, contributing towards your goal of winning an ever greater share of the business you target. The single most effective tool for exploiting losses is the 'De-brief' meeting.

De-briefing is hardly rocket science. All it amounts to is asking the client why you lost their business — and using that information to reduce the possibility that you might lose that way again. Even so, most sellers, even the better ones, do not employ any sort of De-brief mechanism — some because they don't want to dwell on the negative aspects of a loss, and some because they don't feel entitled to ask the client for such feedback. If, however, you make it a goal to improve on the basis of lessons learned from lost business, De-briefs are entirely positive experiences.

As to your right to a client De-brief — think about it: you invested your time, effort and resources in trying to solve your prospect's problem. Surely the least they can do is help you to solve your problem now — your problem being that you need to improve what you do so that a similar loss is unlikely to happen again. You are entitled to a De-brief. Ask for one, every time.

> Turn short-term losses into medium-term wins — always De-brief.

Besides the obvious benefits of offering you an insight into the reasons why you may have lost the business, a De-brief ironically also offers you the opportunity to develop your relationships within the lost account — something that will be extremely useful should you decide to continue your efforts with them. Many people do not like to disappoint, and some client contacts may even feel bad about not giving you their business despite your hard work and professionalism. This can be a great opportunity to develop closer relationships with account contacts.

Running a De-brief

Keep your De-brief meeting short, focused, to-the-point and professional. You want the reasons why you did not win the business, pure and simple. Have a number of questions ready and take copious notes. At a very minimum, include the following:

- Can you detail the particular factors that prompted you to select the successful bidder?

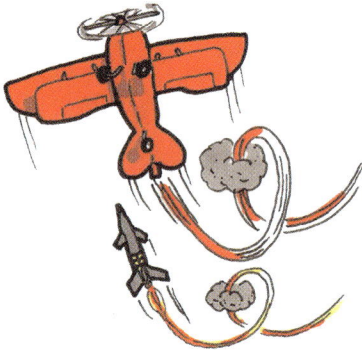

  - If these factors had been present in our proposal, would you have been prepared to do business with us? If not, why not?

  - How else would you suggest that we might have improved our chances of winning your business?

- Would you be prepared to give us copies of non-proprietary parts of the successful vendor's proposal to allow us to analyse more closely why their bid was more successful, helping us to address any shortcomings in our approach to winning future business with your organisation? (Don't be shy of asking for this sort of material — many clients will provide this valuable input to your competitive analysis.)

- Are you prepared to consider us for any future business that might arise? If not, why not?

- Are there any other current requirements that we might be able to help you with?

- Can we stay in touch with you to keep you informed of developments with our company and offerings?

You will find that even the very general questions above will drive the meeting sufficiently to allow you to build a good understanding of why you were unsuccessful.

One of the keys to a successful De-brief is attitude. If you feel too disappointed to follow the general guidelines below, you might do well to forget the idea of a De-brief altogether — you might do more harm than good. So:

- Be pleasant;

- Hold your head high;

- Be the consummate professional;

- Take charge of the De-brief;

- Be careful not to come across as aggressive, bitter or defensive (Disappointed is OK!)

- Pursue discussion of the reasons for your loss until you have a clear understanding;

- Be positive, particularly in your objective that you would like to do some future business with these people;

Many people do not like to disappoint, and some client contacts will feel bad about not awarding you business after a professional effort — this is a relationship-development opportunity.

- Don't be argumentative — stay away from unnecessary detail of any contentious aspects of the prospect's handling of the evaluation process;

- Don't be over-friendly — don't crawl;

265

- Don't allow the conversation to move away from the job at hand to easier general chit-chat until you have the answers for which you came.

Remember that you lost the sale, so don't try to resell. Just get the information you need to ensure that you win next time.

Using the Outcome of Your De-brief

A De-brief is only as useful as the use to which you put what you learn. Be sure to:

1. Share these results with anyone who had input into the unsuccessful proposal and with anyone who may have input into any future sales, particularly in the same account;

2. Brainstorm with your team on how best to address these shortcomings in the future;

3. Put a formal plan in place to address any problem areas, and work it.

Lost sales are the clearest signal that you may be doing something wrong. Problem is, you don't usually know just how wrong until it's too late — until you've invested a large amount of time and effort. Don't just accept losses. Ask for a De-brief to question every one — using anything useful you uncover to reduce the chances that it might happen again.

Remember: Once beaten, twice smart.

Strategy 40

'I Hate Writing Business Proposals'

'I Hate Writing Business Proposals'

...Doesn't Mean I Can't Write Winners

Potential purchasers today have more options than ever before, most of them so closely matched in terms of product/ service performance, quality and price that it is becoming ever more difficult for them to choose between suppliers. Purchasers now routinely call for potential suppliers to prepare proposals for every acquisition that they make, large or small.

If you can't write good proposals, life is going to become more and more difficult for you.

One vital element in improving the quality of your proposals is a compelling framework — a structure for your proposal that sells your ideas and solutions. This strategy introduces the *Winning* proposal framework — a structure that will maximise the success of every future proposal that you write.

Let's Talk Proposals

If, instead of writing a proposal, you were having a one-to-one conversation with your client, trying to *sell* your superior solution to their requirements, you would very likely make the points outlined in this greatly condensed conversation:

> '...we understand your requirements thoroughly...we have a solution to those requirements...this is why our solution is so good for you...here are the costs for our proposed solution...yes, we can prove every claim we've made....'

The most effective business proposals establish precisely this dialogue with their readers, and that's why this *Winning* proposal structure is based upon it. Each element of this conversation suggests a section essential to every business proposal.

'We Understand Your Requirements Thoroughly'

The first thing you absolutely must establish for your client is that you understand their requirements inside out — that you have as detailed an appreciation of what they are trying to achieve as they do themselves (perhaps even better than they do themselves). This is essential.

Many proposal-writers undervalue the persuasive power of re-stating their own understanding of the client requirement — doing an exemplary job of outlining the requirement in your proposals can very often be the difference between winning and losing the target business. Dale Carnegie said that sales success depends upon *'getting them saying "yes, yes" immediately'*. How better

> The most effective business proposals establish an easy dialogue with their readers—drawing the readers in.

269

to do so than confirm the requirements they outlined to you?

The logical first section in your proposal should, therefore, detail the client requirement, and for discussion purposes we will call this section: **The Requirement**.

'We Have a Solution to Those Requirements'

Your first section sets out to convince your client that you have a good understanding of what they are trying to achieve, of their requirements. You now have their attention, so continue your conversation by describing the way in which you can address these requirements — outline your solution. This is the key section of your proposal. You are, after all, writing the proposal to *sell* this solution.

So, your second proposal section should be called something like **The Proposed Solution**.

'This is Why Our Solution is So Good for You'

The client will certainly want to know just what is in your solution for them — what benefits will accrue to them from selection of your solution over that of your competitors.

You must emphasise the particular strengths of your solution, and minimise any weaknesses in it. At the same time, you will also need to highlight any particular weaknesses in likely competitors' solutions, whilst, at the same time, minimising the importance of any strengths they might be able to demonstrate.

> *You must emphasise the particular strengths of your offering.*

This is your third proposal section: **Benefits of the Proposed Solution**.

'Here are the Costs Associated with our Solution'

Now that you have established that you understand the requirement, that you have a good solution to these requirements, and that your solution will be of particular benefit to your client, your client is certainly going to want to know how much this 'best of all possible solutions' is going to cost.

Your fourth section will detail the costs associated with your proposed solution, and, for discussion purposes, we will name it: **Costs**.

'We Can Prove All of the Claims Made in this Proposal'

Up to this point, you have focused on communicating just one basic message — *'We have the best possible solution to your requirements.'* To communicate this message most effectively, you should confine yourself to the main points that support this contention, staying away from excessive detail that might distract the client, drawing their attention off on a tangent.

In each of the sections mentioned above, include only as much detail as is necessary to support the main message that you are trying to communicate with it. All of the detailed technical material — technical specifications, product descriptions, supporting research, and so on — should be confined to appendices at the back of your proposal, with your main text making frequent reference to the presence of this supporting material in the **Appendices** section of your proposal.

271

The Winning Framework for Your Proposals

So, by establishing this simple *Requirements–Solution–Benefits–Costs–Appendices* dialogue with your client in your proposals, you end up with a basic framework for all of your proposals, which will contain at least five sections.

The figure below graphically illustrates this basic proposal model, which you can now use as the basis of all of your future proposals. Besides the self-explanatory *Title Page & Table of Contents*, this figure also contains an additional section that has not yet been discussed — the '**Executive Summary**'.

WINNING PROPOSAL STRUCTURE

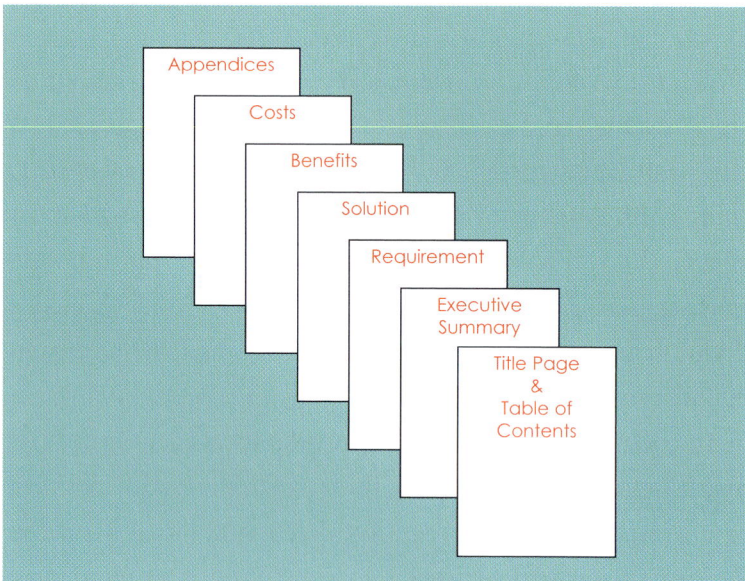

The 'Executive Summary'

The 'Executive Summary' section provides an overview of the total content of your proposal. It is designed for those senior executives in your client organisation who do not have time to consider any more than the 'highlights' of your proposal. It is also designed to be a general introduction for other readers who will wish to read your proposal in its entirety, orienting them on how your proposal is laid out and preparing them for the main points that your proposal will present.

Think of your Executive Summary as the equivalent of what is on the jackets of novels — a quick-to-read summary providing the reader with what they need to 'buy your story'.

Build your Executive Summary using the *Winning* structure — with a few lines summarising each of your completed main sections. Think of the main points that you want each proposal section to make and ensure that these are briefly covered in this summary.

After the Solution section, the Executive Summary is arguably the most important section of any proposal — it may well be the only section that some key readers will bother to read. So, invest the time in getting it right.

Adapt and Thrive

Undoubtedly, some of your proposals will not be of a size that allows you to make your case adequately in just six sections. Similarly, some of your proposals will not be longer than a single letter.

This does not, however, prevent you from using the basic *Executive Summary–Requirements–Solution–Benefits–Costs–Appendices* structure.

A one-page proposal letter should still use the same structure, with brief paragraphs substituting for the sections discussed above. Similarly, larger proposals may demand many more sections, with entirely different titles.

273

The key is to ensure that, however large or small your proposal, you successfully establish this dialogue flow — get your readers saying, 'Yes, yes', throughout.

We can't promise that adopting this structure will result in eliminating your hate of proposal-writing — but we can guarantee that you'll get a vastly higher hit rate for your hated labours.

'*There is nothing to writing. All you do is sit down at a typewriter and open a vein.*'

RED SMITH

Strategy 41

What Do I Do Next?

A Bonus Strategy

Congratulations! You're reading this closing strategy because you've finished reading the forty strategies that make up this book (either that or you're one of those people who always has to read the last few pages of a book first — to see how it ends! If that's the case, then come back here later when you've read the rest!)

I know that, being serious about winning in business, you'll agree that every strategy I've presented here will, at some time or other, play some part in helping you to achieve the victories you seek. However, some of the strategies will be particularly relevant today, some will become particularly relevant tomorrow, and others will only become relevant to you some time in the future. If you're serious about success in business, you'll want to know the best strategy for building these new approaches to key business challenges into your way of winning. So where do you start?

Remember in Strategy 8: Fire 'em Up, how I mentioned that it takes 21 days to change an old habit or create a new one? Use that knowledge. Right now, browse the table of contents and select the five Strategies that are most pertinent to you right now. Now, *commit* that every day for the next 21 days you will review these strategies and ask yourself, 'What can I do today to improve these aspects of the way I run my business and apply the ideas in these strategies?' Truly commit — don't let anything stand in the way of completing this simple but powerful habit-building process. You'll be amazed at the results you'll achieve in this short period.

Then, simply repeat the cycle. If your business is anything like mine, even 21 days will shift the challenges you face so radically that another five of these Strategies will scream out for inclusion in this continuous improvement process.

As I finish this book, I am truly excited about the changes that you are going to make in your business, and the impact that they will have upon you.

I wish you all of the success that you would wish for yourself as you pursue your goal of winning in business.

Deiric McCann
September 2003

Also by Deiric McCann

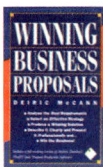

Winning Business Proposals
ISBN: 1-86076-166-6; Paperback
Price: €25.00

In these increasingly competitive times, the difference between winning and losing potential business often comes down to the quality of the business proposal. *Winning Business Proposals* explains the strategies, tactics and techniques that can lead to superior, and successful business proposals, and provides a step-by-step guide to the entire proposal-writing process.

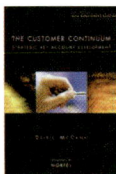

The Customer Continuum
Strategic Key Account Management
ISBN: 1-86076-096-1; Paperback
Price: €45.00

Not all customers are created equal. Some merit your time and effort, others do not. Key account development is time-consuming and expensive, and can be justified only if the potential returns are sufficient to warrant the effort. So how do you tell which accounts are going to be profitable before you invest in them? This Briefing provides the answers.

Available from:
Oak Tree Press, 19 Rutland Street, Cork, Ireland
Tel: +353 (0) 21 431 3855; Fax: +353 (0) 21 431 3496
Email: info@oaktreepress.com